Why Trump & America Have Already Won!

Why the 2016 Republican Primaries will Make History

By David Peters

Disclaimer

I would like to say right from the very start that this book is not written by a pundit or political expert. These are my opinions and my opinions only and you can either agree with them or not as you see fit. I have done my best to separate the truth from the political spin game and honestly believe that I have done a good job. I have also done my best to provide accurate information although some information is bound to change over time. So read the book for informational purposes but please, do not cast any bets at the local bar based on specifics.

Contents

Introduction

I believe that before you read this book that you know a little bit about myself. Not because I am a unique or utterly interesting fellow but because how I look at certain things is influenced by the type of person I have become in life. For the reason alone, here goes.

I am in my 60's which means that over the course of my existence I have witnessed at least 15 presidential elections. To be totally fair there were a few I was not aware of due to my youth, several more I didn't care about also due to my youth and more than a few that were so boring I didn't follow them at all.

But that all changed this year for several reasons that will be discussed throughout this book.

I am not a political expert and you will not find a slew of historical references or endless pontificating on how what we are seeing now relates to elections back in the 1800's. I am more interested in what is happening now and how it is going to affect our future in this country.

I should also state that there is some bias in this book as I have several strong opinions on what is happening now in our political system and how it is going to impact the election and the future of our country. I do honestly believe that the time has come for change especially after the mockery of a government we have been subjected to over the last decade. I am specifically talking about government shut downs and little of anything of substance happening because of party rhetoric and stubbornness.

I am not a Hillary fan and both her recent past and her past with her husband while he was president and all their legal issues and troubles make me naturally skeptical of her abilities and motivation. Plus, I get the feeling that she panders a whole heck of a lot and talks down to people like you and I in her speeches and debates. Again, this is my personal opinion so please do not be offended.

As far as the republicans were concerned there were so many candidates at one time they all could not fit on the same debate stage so they had to have an "A" debate and a "B" debate to fit everyone in. No one wanted to be in the "B" debate and candidates dropped like flies over the first month or so.

But it was during those debates that I became interested at first and then fascinated by what I was watching and how the people and the process were going on around me.

At times I laughed while at other times I was ashamed and even disgusted by what I saw and read. But as the process went on and on I soon realized that this was just like a chess game where candidates made their moves trying to establish each of them as a front runner or legitimate candidate.

I also realized that I could listen to two or three candidates who would take the same issue or statement and spin it so it made sense for whatever their point of view was. I found some of this amusing while at other times I felt it was insulting. I mean, while I might not be the most intelligent guy in the room at any given time, I am smart enough to know BS when I hear it. And there was a lot of it flying around.

For me personally I realized that throughout this process my eyes and ears where being made aware of things I had never known or even been aware of. Certain things that on the surface appeared nice and friendly while at their roots they were something totally different and insidious. All put there to benefit a group of people running the show behind the scenes.

After a while I realized that I had been seeing things that were never seen before during any election in my lifetime or at least my memory. I was seeing more of how things really were instead of how certain people and organizations wanted me to see them and that's a good thing.

I also saw pettiness and vindictiveness and at times outright childishness. But at the root of every comment and inappropriate gesture or topic, I saw the strategy beneath it and I found myself predicting, accurately I might add, what was going to happen next. Not as a political analyst or expert but instead as someone observing a game or a deal and working through it.

So excuse any prejudice that might come through on these pages because it will probably come out as I discuss what I saw and how I interpreted it. This is largely my thoughts and feeling and like I said, most of them turned out to be right or at least reasonable.

But despite everything that has happened and all the times I wondered where the heck we were heading towards I think there will be strong positive things resulting by this entire process. I am not being cynical when I say there will be books written about this whole process for years and you can bet your life there will be changes before the next election in 2020. Changes that will come about out of protests and transparency not because either party sought to be more transparent and fair.

Finally, as a point of reference, I am writing this book during the time that the Republicans have reduced their candidates to Trump, Kasich and Cruz. The Democrats have their Hillary and Bernie Sanders. As I am writing this we are mostly through the primary process and have just finished the New York Primary.

There are about 10-12 states to go and talk about a contested convention (which makes everything even murkier) is all the hope for two of the three Republicans.

So please keep an open mind as you read this book. I feel it is an open and honest evaluation of what's going on and while you might disagree with several things you read, you cannot deny that this is all happening. Depending on how your favorite candidates might be your views might be the same or similar to mine or they might be completely different. But so has this entire election process so why should anything change now?

Ok, let's get started!

The Perfect Storm

Very few things in life happen in a vacuum. The vast majority of time things happens now because of other things that happened in the past. Even if those things seemingly appear unrelated, they still can have a significant effect on current events. This most certainly has been the case when it comes to this election season.

When you stop and think about it, so many things had to happen before and during this entire process to get us to this point. While I am fairly certain that I will miss a few of the contributing factors, here are some of the events and attitudes that have brought us to this 2016 election process:

The Past 8-12 Years

For most people, attitudes are not changed by a single action or situation. Most people require a sustained pattern of events that first get them to realize certain things are happening and from that point their interest is piqued.

From that point that might start paying a bit more attention or just become more aware of everything that is happening around them. In other words they now see what has been in front of them over the last few years.

At this point is when anger and frustration begin to set in. they look at everything with a more cynical point of view and they are no longer content to let things stay the same. Their frustration moves to anger and anger hopefully leads to action. The longer this happens or goes on the stronger the reaction and the louder the voice for change becomes.

Anger & Frustration

Most people expect their government to exist to support them in developing infrastructure and support services as well as to keep them and the country safe on the world stage. This is what they expect when they vote someone into office. They want and expect these elected officials to be their voice in government.

But over the last 8-12 years they have not seen that in their government. They have seen gridlock at time so severe that the entire government was shut down with many people shut out of their jobs and unable to pay their living expenses.

This kind of activity was almost comical at times with people from both sides refusing to budge an inch and playing politics with people's lives.

People also saw these elected representatives with their Cadillac benefit plans and expense accounts acting more on their own personal interests than in representing the people who elected them. Whether accurate or not the perception in the minds of most people was that their interests no longer mattered the most. Instead the elected officials were more concerned in their own future than the future of the country.

Party Politics

For the last several years the two party system has resulted in so much aggression and confrontation that it ceased to operate in a beneficial manner. Decisions made almost totally along party lines meant that little or nothing was accomplished. Republicans ridiculed anything created by a Democrat and Democrats rejected anything offered by a Republican. Co-operation between the parties became less and less frequent and is now a rarity.

The problem with this is that many, if not most, of the problems and troubles of the lower and middle class are not just a Republican or a Democratic problem.

These things effect people of both parties and in all areas of the country. But the entire system has succeeded in making these party issues which they intend to fight and not issues of the people that they want to solve.

The other thing that has been made extremely obvious over the last several months is that both parties were almost totally out of contact with the people they represent. They had little to no idea how people really felt about their government or the degree or level of anger that was out there in our cities and towns. They finally realized that both parties had placed their own interests and agenda ahead of the needs of the people.

Taxes & Finances

When it comes to government, taxes, debt and waste are the three primary concerns of the people. They are constantly seeing their income taxes and property taxes rise and in many areas of the country the services and benefits they receive being decreased. The end result is that almost everyone is paying more and getting less and they don't like it.

They also see a lack of financial restraint and an inequity of whatever sacrifice is asking to be made.

The upper 1% is making all the money while paying just a fraction of the taxes that they should be paying. So the lower and middle class are asked to pay more and receive less and to be happy about it in the process.

People are also expecting government to use their tax money wisely to provide the most value for their money. But this is simply not done due to special interests and elected officials not exercising the same judgment and values as they would with their own personal income.

We have all heard the stories of the $500 hammers and lavish expense reports and these things breed discontent with the rest of the people struggling from paycheck to paycheck.

World Politics

The world is a big place full of different people, different languages and different agendas. There are countries who have religious differences and agendas and other countries looking to expand or cause problems for other countries. In some cases there are mild difference and in other cases extreme hatred between countries and cultures.

Much of this is out of our expertise and we elect people we feel have the knowledge and experience to be able to interact with these different people and cultures to create a spirit of cooperation and balance within the world.

The problem is that we do not see this working and many people feel that as a country we are being asked to do more than our fair share and that we are being taken advantage of in the process. People are losing their jobs as companies move overseas to save money and government seems OK that this kind of activity continues.

Trade deals with other countries are often one sided with our country getting the worst end of the deal. We pay more or charge no tariffs on in-coming good while other countries tax our goods coming into their countries. So the result is that foreign goods cost less in our country while our good are seeing their prices inflated to where that countries products are less expensive. It is not a fair deal and we are being taken advantage of.

One significant aspect of world politics is that we appear to be vulnerable to attacks because as a country we do little to stop those people responsible. We are so caught up in being politically correct and placating every single person with an opinion that we have created a culture where any kind of action or response is met with protests and civil unrest.

Party Self-Interest

Though it should not come as a surprise for anyone, both parties are structured so that they perform and act in the party's best interests even though they might not align with the interests of the American people. One very positive thing that has arisen from this election process is that this has been brought out of the back room closets and placed in full view of the people.

While this might be thought of as a cynical attitude by some politicians, I can only point to the government dysfunction and gridlock over the years as proof that what is good for the people is not what necessarily is best for the parties.

I full believe that if a Republican came up with a cure for cancer the Democrats would fight it and vice versa. I just base this opinion on what has transpired over the last several years and how it has impacted so many people at the expense of the ego's and agendas of certain politicians.

Special Interests

I hate special interests. The very idea that the interests of a multi-national conglomerate or big oil or big pharma should be more important than the needs of middle class Americans is lost on me like it is lost on most people.

But despite my disgust, special interests control a great deal of what happens in our government despite the protests to the contrary.

We have banks that disrupt the financial system for their own gain at the expense of people like you and I. People lost their homes or their retirement savings while the people who engaged in the activity and the banks themselves get slapped on the wrist at worst.

We have health care companies raking in huge and obscene profits while people spend more and more of their savings on grossly over-priced medications. Medications in this country and priced higher than anywhere else because we allow it to happen.

Lobbyists spend millions and millions of dollars "buying" politicians through campaign contributions thus tying their personal success to the success of the special interests. Other special interests control such a huge number of people that their votes alone will control how a politician reacts and votes.

Take for example the National Rifle Association, the supreme gun rights organization that sees no difference in people owning a hand gun for self-defense and owning a 45 shot assault rifle or several of them for the same reason.

These are the people who believe that people should be able to purchase and own special "cop killer" ammunition that can pierce a bullet proof vest!

Who do you think is behind the total inability to set limits on gun ownership or at least make it more difficult for people with a history of mental problems or other problems to get a license? Why do you think various politicians vote against these laws? Because they are controlled by the special interests.

Tell that to the families of people who have lost loved ones at the hands of some jackass with an assault weapon. People do not ask for 100% perfection in what happen within the government. They just do not want to see the rights of a few and the success of a corporation take on a higher value than the rights of the people.

Housing & the Mortgage Bust

In the previous decade we saw the age of entitlement come to light and the big banks were lining up to get people mortgages to buy homes they could not afford. Then the banks sold these high risk loans to investors and when people were unable to keep up with the payments they lost their homes and the investors were left loans that were in default. But the banks who had sold these loans had made their profits and left with smiles on their faces.

Tens of thousands of people lost their homes and life savings in the process and the problem was so widespread it started a recession later on in the decade that crippled the economy and cost many people their jobs. Just recently fines were levied against the last of these big banks but those fines will not give people their homes back and the fines themselves became tax deductions so the fines were not nearly as large as they seemed in the first place.

People became outraged that these banks and Wall Street could be so powerful and do so much against the law without fear of repercussions that they become almost totally disenfranchised with the process. This was seen as yet another way for the rich and powerful to cheat the lower and middle classes with the help of the government and those who were elected to serve and protect the American people.

Deception and Spin Cycles

My mother did not raise a genius or a Rhodes Scholar but she did raise someone with more than a little bit of common sense. I can listen to most anything and understand what people are saying although at times I might have to go online to read up on something to really understand it.

But I have to say that I now believe that being rational and using common sense has no place in the political process or in the election process as well. In fact, it is a good thing that DVR's have a rewind and fast forward button so I could stop and go back to re-listen to something I just listened to that made my head explode.

For example, I have heard a candidate running a very distant third who was mathematically out of the race tell his supporters he was in the best position to capture the nomination! Then another candidate claiming that he won the last 14 elections when in reality he won 3 elections and 11 district contests!

Finally, one candidate stated that his campaign was the only campaign that has steadily shown that they could beat another candidate. But the reality was that they had lost 20 states and won just 10!

These comments or statements are by no means unique as politicians have been "spinning" the facts and the truth for decades. But the difference is now people are sick and tired of it and the longer it continues the more people get tired of it. People want to make their choices and decisions based on truth and not how one person spins the truth to meet their own agenda.

Depending on the people or persons involved, there could very well be a lot more factors and examples on why we find ourselves in the state that our country finds itself in right now. But make no mistake about it, we would not have the remaining candidates we have had government been a finely tuned and high-function process in the eyes of the people. You can agree or disagree on some of the things mentioned in this chapter but you simply have to agree that all of this has brought us to the point we all find ourselves at.

At that is not necessarily a bad thing.

Politically Incorrect

One of the problems are have in this world right now is our fascination and preoccupation with being politically correct. Not just to the extent of controlling hate speech or inappropriate humor or similar things but to the point where we have become afraid to refer to anything or everything as exactly what it is.

Like many other things that have occurred over the years we have gone from one extreme to another. While there were days when people openly discriminated against certain groups of people today we seem to be searching for terms and expressions and reading into them things that just do not exist. Sometimes this allows the true message from being expressed.

At the same time we have developed a type of "sterile language" that attempts to sanitize our language so that it does not offend a single soul. While this is admirable at the same time it changes who we are and at the same time changes the messages we send to each other.

The comedian George Carlin had a routine that talked about this very thing.

He talked about how we go to great lengths to make things appear less serious than they really are. The example he used was a military example of what happens when a solider gets so overwhelmed in battle that his emotional system ceases to function normally.

In World War One they called it "shell shock". But this was determined to be too violent and serious so it was changed "battle fatigue" in later wars. This term made it seem less serious and less frightening. But eventually even this was changed to the current "post-traumatic stress disorder" which doesn't really give you much of an insight as to what the problem even is anymore.

We have a President today that has a problem calling terrorism by the actual name terrorism and refuses to accept or admit that there is a segment of the world's population that is responsible for this activity. Yet people keep dying and families keep losing their sons and daughter and we are more interested in being politically correct than actually identifying and solved the problem.

Then a candidate like Donald Trump comes along and is not afraid to say what he really thinks even if it offends people or hurts their feelings. In reality he was saying things out loud that a lot of people had been thinking to themselves about for years.

This resonated with a large percentage of people because it was something they never heard before.

Sure it alienated people as well but it was something so different and so unique that he developed a very strong following from people who had reached their limit and wanted to see things changed and no longer ignored. Not everyone agreed with everything he said or even how he said it but they wanted to hear his message.

As I watched this unfold I would cringe at something that were said and was certain that his last statement would be his undoing. But he took on politics and religion and different groups of people who were part of the problems the country was experiencing and every comment or stand seemed not to hurt him but instead cause his support to become stronger and deeper.

A side benefit of this type of activity was that he became instantly more newsworthy. Everyone wanted him on his show or to have him grant them an interview. They wanted the latest sound bite or something that could be played all day on CNN or other networks. He easily outpaced the amount of air time he was given as compared to other candidates. Whether this was part of a well thought out marketing program or just a welcome surprise, it worked out very well for him.

But at the same time the world has become constantly more critical and finding more and more things to complain about. They complained about the Tomahawk Chop at Atlanta Braves games. It wasn't meant to ridicule Indians or make fun of them. It was meant to be a fun thing for the crowd to do to interact with the game.

When I go to a Yankee game I do not think about the conflict between the North and South, I think about a baseball team and not about a white versus black issue. The Washington Redskins have been around for decades but now their name is racist. Go figure. I don't see it.

Right now the world has some real problems it needs to act upon. We have terrorism and ISIS. We have unstable people and countries getting nuclear weapons and we have people who seem to think it is perfectly acceptable to walk into a school with an assault weapon and kill our sons and daughters. These are real problems. When we get all of this and a few other things under control then we can revisit this politically correct stuff.

One of the reasons why I think that even if he loses either the Republican nomination or the race for the Presidency, Donald Trump has already won and achieved at least part of what he set out to do. He has raised the awareness of the people when it comes to certain things that have always been hidden in the closet or under the sheets and kept from us.

He is not afraid to call out problems and poor behavior as he sees it. He is not afraid to point out inequalities or the agendas of other people and other groups. A lot of people have found this new, different and even a tad refreshing. Others have found it offensive and threatening to their way of life.

All of my life I have had a hard time with what certain people call prejudice. I always wondered how someone could be called prejudicial if they made their judgments and choices based on real life experiences.

I mean if I am walking down the street and I get mugged by a blue man and beaten and the next day I see another person suffer the same conflict with another blue man and then I hear on the news that a blue man attacked a grandmother in the same neighborhood, is it prejudicial to cross the street to walk on the other side when a blue man is walking towards me? If I stand at an intersection and watch 15 cars fail to stop at a stop sign am I wrong to think the next two cars aren't going to stop either? Would I be wrong to think that the next car is likely to run the stop sign or should I just walk in front of it to cross the street anyway?

While I understand that it is wrong to discriminate against anyone or any group of people, I also understand that identifying threats and catching the people responsible is vitally important to our nation's security as well as our personal security. But it appears that our security is less important than possibly offending someone.

Law enforcement agencies such as the FBI and their sister organizations in other countries use profiling of various degrees in most of their investigations. Not because they hate Muslims or Black people or any particular group but because it allows them to zero in on the most likely suspect or allows them to focus on the right areas to help them catch the perpetrators. Are there "bad apples" in these organizations? Yes. Are there people who are biased against certain groups? Yes. But you should not eliminate a beneficial activity because of a few people.

Today we have become a nation afraid to speak our mind and say what needs to be said. We sanitize everything in the hopes of saying the right thing to the right people at the right time so as not to create controversy or even to cause a lawsuit. In the meantime, problems that are there right under our noses and effecting the lives of our people and the security of our nation are going unresolved.

The other thing we have to deal with is that our nation plays by rules that other nations just don't care about and while they have no problem doing certain things to us, we find those same things abhorrent and refuses to respond in kind. In many cases this makes us appear weak in the eyes of other countries and I am sure some people in the world laugh at us for it.

While I am not saying that we should lower ourselves to the ideals of others or turn our country and its values into something different, I do realize that a few people with idealistic and unreasonable values should not dictate how the entire nations behaves or responds. Yet you will not find a group of people in our government willing to say this out loud in front of a microphone.

Donald Trump shocked more than a few people and made some unpopular statements about terrorism and our border problems and illegal immigration. It wasn't that these problems were brand new or shocking to us but many people were not aware of the magnitude of some problems and how they effected us as a country and as people.

While many groups and organizations condemned Trump's comments and other twisted them around into political rhetoric, people responded because he had spoken thoughts and ideas that were in the heads of millions of people but left unsaid but those statements were not politically correct.

These statements both hurt Trump and helped him gain a following of like-minded people who were also tired of having to make everything they said politically correct and sanitized. It caused many people to fear Trump but many others to join his supporters. Not everything was right or smart for him to say because some of the comments were unduly harsh but most of them needed to be said.

You do not have to agree with his views or his statements but you have to applaud him having the guts to say them out loud in front of millions of people.

The importance of having the courage to make these statements and say what needs to be said is that it creates controversy which brings along discussion. It helps bring issues and problems more out in the open so that people like you and I become aware of them and the impact they could have on our lives. Most of us are not aware of everything that goes on around us and if the people we elect to represent us do not speak openly and candidly about these things, we just make those problems better and more difficult to solve.

I am not saying that people should feel free to insult other groups of people or discriminate against them. But what I am saying is that we should be more determined to discuss issues and things as they really are instead of misrepresenting them by carefully choosing our words and comments to avoid offending someone who just maybe needs to be offended once in a while.

Not Taken Seriously

If the candidates running for the Republican nomination could have a "do-over" and go back in time for a year they most certainly would accept that offer. Because no one saw the writing on the wall when it came to one particular candidate that would set the entire party on its ear.

There had been rumors before about Donald Trump running for President of the United States. In previous elections he would raise the possibility but nothing happened. It was thought of as a public relations ploy to get his name back in the papers or on the national news casts. So when the rumors came about this year, no one thought there was anything to them.

Even when he made the announcement that he was really serious and when he made his announcement that he was indeed running in this election his candidacy was not taken seriously. It was thought he would quickly disappear as the voters would pick established politicians that really knew what government and politics was really about.

No one thought that someone without political experience could compete, let alone be even somewhat successful when they had to go up against some of the most well-known and popular political figures. No one gave Trump or a few other candidates a chance of becoming successful.

This was not an unreasonable opinion in that candidates such as Carly Fiorino, Ben Carson and Trump were not politicians. They had little experience in making political speeches or in getting people to support them or even standing up in a debate against people who had been doing these same things for years or even decades.

I liken this to a bully in school who was so much bigger than someone that he thought picking on the smaller boy was going to be an easy fight until the smaller boy beat the crap out of him when it came time to fight. But that is exactly what has happened so far in this primary battle. No one thought Trump would be a serious candidate but they were mistaken.

The thing is whenever you underestimate someone you usually do not pay much attention to what they are doing or what is happening until it is possibly too late. By the time you do realize that you had better take the person seriously they have already established themselves or have built a following that cannot be easily dismissed.

We will talk about this in more detail later on but it was the arrogance of a few of the candidates as well as the entire Republican Party leadership that failed to see what was happening right before their eyes. They failed to see the momentum even as it started and their arrogance convinced them that this kind of growth or following could not be sustained and all they had to do was wait it out.

With two month left in the primary process they are still waiting.

As I watched the early series of debates you could easily see that no one thought that they had anything to fear from Trump. The so-called "leading candidates" concentrated more on eliminating those candidates they perceived to be a much greater threat while pretty much dismissing Trump and leaving him alone.

While I can easily see why this would have happened early on in these debates I was surprised to see this continue even as Trump established himself as time went on. By the time other candidates turned their attention to Trump it was too late as he had already established a following that would only grow moving forward.

Though it is so much easier to evaluate things after they happened I found it interesting to see how a candidate like Trump could parlay his candidacy into a front-runner by initially flying under the radar while capitalizing on the arrogance of those involved in the system.

He didn't complain about it or mention it. He just took advantage of it and appeared on countless new programs advancing his campaign while other concentrated on other candidates.

By the time others began taking him seriously it was too late for several of them. The field of candidates steadily decreased and the one candidate most people thought would be an early casualty of the system remained strong. I think this will be a mistake that will not be made again either by a candidate or the parties themselves because now they have seen first-hand how arrogance and misplaced self-importance can back fire when applied to the wrong candidate.

Unresponsive Party

While it has certainly been no secret that our government has not functioned at a high level as far as protecting the interests of the people is concerned, it is amazing just how disconnected both political parties have become over the years.

The Republican Party, for example, had lost so much contact with their party members and their roots that they had little idea just how strong emotions were when it came to government. Even more shocking was that they had no idea how much their members would respond to a non-politician such as Trump or Ben Carson.

Make no mistake about it a candidate like Donald Trump never would have initially been accepted or welcomed into the political arena had it not been for this disgust and outright anger of the American people. And that anger never would have reached the level it has had the Republican Party bothered to care about how the American voter really felt.

Stop for a moment and think about the last 8-12 years where Democrat blocked Republican and Republican blocked Democrat.

Think about the issues that didn't get addressed and the problems that were not only allowed to remain but often grew larger and more serious as time went by. Think about the government shut downs that kept thousands of people from feeding their families and for many government services to remain closed.

But this was not just a Republican issue as the Democrats were willing accomplices in this governmental farce as well. They are by no means innocents and the rise of Bernie Sanders plays to those same feelings of anger and frustration as well. So there really is a ton of blame to go around.

Had the parties really cared about their voters and how they felt about their government leadership, they would have taken action to reduce the problems and control the anger. But they didn't make the effort. Instead they allowed their arrogance to lead their way and they continued to think that the only thing that truly mattered was how the party looked after its own interests instead of the interests of the people.

But along came Donald Trump and Ben Carson and other outsiders and for once these "outsiders" had a forum in which they could use their voice to inform the American people. For once they had a platform where they could reveal what had been so carefully hidden from the voters and bring it all out in the open.

The interesting thing is that these feelings and situations do not occur overnight. They build gradually over time as people see other acting in an unprofessional manner, not doing their job and not seeing any repercussions for their actions. They get angry because if the average citizen refused to do their job or fought and blocked everything they didn't agree with that they would lose their jobs.

But the one thing that people hate more than anything is being made to feel like they don't matter and that is exactly what both parties have managed to do. From their party dominated delegated system to their arrogance regarding to the needs of the people the parties have failed to properly and effectively represent the people.

The way "outsiders" of any type get their foot through the door is through the discontent of others. Almost everyone realizes this and the political parties should have realized this as well. But discontent opened the door and candidates like Trump and Carson walked through the open door.

This will have a lasting effect as well because anyone associated with the "establishment" or current government will be branded as being part of the problem instead of part of a possible solution. So the politicians of the group, Jeb Bush, Marco Rubio and Chris Christy had huge mountains to climb just to gain acceptance.

Remember, whenever you allow something to open the door, you sometimes have little control over who or what walks through it. I am fairly sure neither party will want to go through a repeat of this year's events any time soon.

Loyal Following

One very interesting phenomenon in this election has been the following of supporters that Trump has created. Not only have these people rallied behind Trump but they have been intensely loyal and it has been almost impossible for Trump to say or do anything that would cause his supporters to turn to other candidates.

Even when he openly challenged the Pope or had multiple opinions on the same subject within hours or each other or when he uttered various cringe worthy statements, his supporters stayed with him. Even during times when people swore that he went too far or said something too controversial his poll numbers didn't go down, instead they went up!

This has shown that Trump supporters are bound by some deep commitment or that they somehow resonate with Trump because he seems to speak their language and say what is on their minds. It appears that they so desperately want someone who understands them to speak for them and up until now that person has not existed.

I also think they appreciate and respond to Trump because he does not talk or act like a politician. He does not answer questions, or better yet avoid questions, like a politician is trained to do. He does not have 50 different views on issues depending on which state he is talking to at the time. We have said this before but you don't have to agree with what he says but you have to know it comes from the heart.

It is also an interesting dynamic that somehow people feel that a multi-billionaire somehow understands how the working man and woman feels. But even though he lives a lifestyle far more extravagant than most people, you get the idea that he does understand what is fueling our fears and anger.

In watching the debates, all of which I found very interesting for many reasons, I found him to be the most sincere although at time insincere. I also liked the fact that if he didn't like something or someone he said it openly. He did not hide behind phony comments or politically correct jargon. In other words, he said what was on his mind and nothing short of it.

He also made some "misstatements and verbal mistakes but in many ways when he admitted to them or changed his mind he became more human and more like us in some ways. He didn't try to distort the truth like Ted Cruz or endlessly bring up what a rough childhood he had or anything like that.

Sometimes the admissions were a bit sketchy but for the most part, he admitted, often much later though, that perhaps he should not have done something or done something differently.

All of these factors plus many others that resonated with the people have helped him create not just a loyal following but a passionate one as well. And sometimes this has led him straight into trouble.

The nature of Trump's delivery and message can be more than a bit insightful and emotional. Early on in the campaign he made a few ill-advised comments about hecklers or protesters and mentioned that he would like to "punch that guy in the face" and similar comments. The problem was that some of his supporters and followers took that literally and the result was violence at his rally's and events.

This of course became an issue with the other candidates who were quick to take Trump to task for his incendiary comments and rhetoric. They pounced on this saying that Trump thrives on hate and violence in his campaign even though that was not the truth. This is what happens when you say things without thinking which unfortunately happened frequently early on.

One interesting thing was that everyone says that Trump does well with uneducated people or people without college degrees.

What I find interesting is that the more you look into what he is saying most of the time, you see that there is truth behind the statements. Contrast this to the fact twisting and distorted views of Ted Cruz and Hillary Clinton. Because of this one might think that the more educated the voter the more they would see behind the fact spin that is rampant in politics.

While I do not agree with everything Trump has said, and he has made many mistakes both in comments and judgment over these last few months, I find it interesting that no one such as the other candidates, or anything such as the Super PAC's anti-Trump ads, seems to be able to shake loose Trump supporters. While they might be having an impact on getting new voters into the fold, their efforts in reducing Trumps sizeable following have failed miserably.

I also think this worries the Republican Party because if they somehow find a way to deny Trump the nomination through back office deals or other means, Trump could very well take his run to a third party and bring all of these people along with him. That has to be a very real concern for the party and their hopes of beating Hillary in November.

Trump the Salesman

For anyone with sales experience or has been trained or educated in sales, this election has new meaning. Because you can see Trump's "performance" and approach as a classic sales process. Virtually everything he has done has been part of a process to connect the voter to the "product" in this case being the candidate.

While most candidates follow pretty much the same process because they want the voters to choose them over other candidates, some accomplished this objective easier than others. Most people do well in some areas and not so well in others while some of the least effective candidates failed to do several important things in order to connect with the voters.

Here are the steps in the process and how Trump captured and used those steps to create his support with the voters:

Know Your Audience

This is where both parties, and several candidates went almost totally unaware. Most candidates realized that people were not happy with the government but none, except Trump, realized to what extent that anger and frustration had risen to.

Trump and his people understood the people. He knew what people were thinking and feeling probably because he has businesses that are all over the country and because he employs so many people. In some respects he had resources that no other candidate had as far as identifying and understanding how the people felt.

Knowing and understand how and what the people are feeling allows the candidate to tap into those feelings and emotions and address them individually and personally. This allows a person, in this case the candidate, to reach people effectively and on a deeper level while at the same time capturing more of their attention and support.

It is important to understand that this information was out there waiting to be discovered. Elected officials and party people did not really look into this or particular care how the people felt. They were so wrapped up in their own party and their own interests they failed to tap into what the people were really feeling. That is what opened the door for Trump in the first place.

Find and Understand the Problems

If you want someone to do something for you or support you it is critical that you give them a reason to do so. While some candidate seemed to feel the voters should be thankful for their presence and while other candidates tried to rely on past achievements or family heritage, Trump and a few other candidates actually talked about the issues that were personally impacting the lives of the voters.

When you identify and understand the issues and problems you get a huge insight into what message you need to deliver and how to deliver it in the most effective manner. The more you can include and promote the real problems and issues to the people the more people are going to listen to you.

This was one thing where both Cruz and Trump excelled early on. Kasich and Christie and Rubio did as well but their method of delivering their message and how they performed caused them to become less effective. But Cruz and Trump focused on the people and the issues and even though they had drastically different styles and approaches, they were effective early on in the process.

Get the Attention of the People

In sales, you are always looking to capture the interest of the people as quickly as possible. The longer it takes for you to capture their interests the higher chance you have of losing those people for good.

You capture the attention of the people by basically doing two things. Have a message that they can relate to and interests them and delivering that message in as entertaining manner as possible so they remain interested and engaged. It is when you nail both of those parts that your message is both heard and understood.

Trump, through his actions and comments has both captured the initial interest of the voters while providing entertainment at the same time. You can either agree with him or be against what he is saying but the fact that you tune in to hear or watch the latest meeting or statement means he has accomplished his goal. He has got your attention.

In many ways capturing the attention of the voter is even more important than your initial message especially in the early stages of a campaign. Before you can get someone to really listen you have to make them want to listen. This is where Trump has excelled. This is where he has separated himself from the rest of the pack.

Yes, he has been outrageous and yes, he has said a few things that made a lot of people cringe. But at the same time he has also said a lot of things that needed to be said and those have resonated remarkably well with the public. But as far as getting people to pay attention to him and building his brand as a candidate I truly believe that no one has done this better.

Connect the Problems to the People

Since this chapter is about being a salesman and using selling and sales principles, let's discuss another thing that Trump has managed to do very effectively since the start of the campaign. That is connecting the problems of the people with the people themselves.

The sales people who close the most sales have something in common with the candidates who attract the largest following. They are not content just to talk about the issues and the problems. They take things a step further. A very important step further. They not only state the problem but they connect those problems to the people so they are aware of the effects these problems and issues have on their personal lives.

This is important because a candidate has to create a favorable impression or perception in the mind of the voter. Not only that but they have to make sure the voter is engaged enough to actually take action and vote. Voting takes time and effort and many people will only vote if they feel it is in their best interests to do so.

A lot of people in politic talk in broad statements and expect the voters to connect the problem with the needs or impact on the voters. But whenever you leave that connection up to the voter or other people you run the risk of that connection never being properly made.

Trump takes a problem and then customizes and personalizes it to the area where he is speaking. For example, other candidates might come into a state and talk about job loss and the economy. Trump will come in and make it personal. He will talk about specific local companies who have left for overseas. He will mention specific numbers of jobs and specific local incomes of the residents of those states. He will tie companies leaving to lower salaries and higher unemployment. He will make it sound more real and more personal.

One of the knocks against Trump is the lack of specifics when it comes to issues and resolving problems. But the fact is people at this point of the process do not need specific answers to their problems. They just want to know that their problems matter and that they are on the candidate's agenda or radar.

While Trump has been outrageous and has said some pretty over the top and sometimes offensive comments, many of those comments were needed to be said to get dialogue flowing in areas that were previously deemed off-limits. But by connecting those comments with real problems and connecting those problems with real people he established a strong connection between him and his supporters.

Offer Solutions to the Problems

All the candidates were in agreement when it comes to one thing. People also want answers to their problems and concerns. But the candidates differ as to what kind of answers those voters really want.

Most people do not need, and do not want, long rambling answers loaded with political phrasing and complicated language and policies. Instead, what most people are looking for are candidates who assess a certain importance and priority to their needs. They just want to be relatively sure that the candidate they vote for has their best interests at heart.

Other candidates throughout the primaries have condemned Trump because they say he has little substance. That his ideas have little or no action steps or plans behind them. They claim that the public wants details and specifics as to how he is going to do those things he says he will do.

But the real fact is that people do not necessarily want or need all those details. If a candidate states that getting companies to move back to this country from overseas, they really don't want to know how this is going to be done only that it is done so there will be more jobs for Americans and more money coming back to this country. They are more interested in results than they are in details.

Trump has made a point to mention the main problems the country and its people are facing and he has made comments as to what he felt was important and what he was going to do about it. It is obvious that his comments and approach are being supported as he has over a 3,000,000 individual vote lead over Cruz and roughly 6,000,000 over Kasich.

The candidates might be obsessing over details but it is clear that the voters are far more interested in results than the details of how they are going to get those results. And what the people feel is what is ultimately important.

Closing the Deal

At some point in the sales process you get to the point where you sum up everything you have said or done to date and look to close the deal. In politics the closing of the deal refers to getting people to make a commitment to voting for you. Everything else is secondary when it comes to capturing the vote of the people.

As the individual state elections get closer and closer, each candidate will take all of their issues and agendas and try to close the deal and capture the vote. Every one of Trumps rallies and television appearances is designed to capture a vote.

To make him appear to be the best candidate with the best chance of improving the life of the people.

Closing the deal is the last part of the sales process where you tie everything together with a huge bow and ask the people for their vote. This is where we show the voter what their vote for you will mean for them and how you represent the best chance for positive change in their country, state or town.

There is an art to doing this. Some candidates try to do this far too early while other might wait a bit too long. Some never get to this point for one reason or another. One reason I think Trump has done so well with this is that he has several decades of business experience behind him that give him the ability to understand both the voter and the political system. This enables him to navigate through the process with far more intuition and success than most other candidates.

I do not mean to equate courting votes to selling products on the internet or referring to voters as customers or candidates as products. It has been my intention to show how the vote getting process is so close to a sales process that some candidates are able to adapt business skills very well in a political system.

I hope after reading this chapter you will see the same parallels that I do when it comes to sales and politics. At least it is another way to look at and understand the political process.

Bringing in the People

One problem both parties have today is getting the people to vote. Dissatisfaction with Washington and overall voter apathy is keeping people away from the polls and away from the political system. Many people feel disenfranchised because they feel the system is not designed for their benefit but for the politicians instead. Even those voters who are frustrated and angry see no path for change so they feel "Why vote"?

It might interest you to know that in 2008, voter turnout as a very poor level of 62.3 percent of eligible voters. In 2012 that level dipped even lower to 57.5% meaning just a little bit more than half of the voters actually voted. Even though the population increased by over 8 million people between 2008 and 2012 turnout actually declined over those years.

Another interesting fact was that in the two elections prior to 2008 there was a slight increase in voter turnout. This all points to dissatisfaction and anger over the way the government has functioned over the last 8 years and how the general public related to our government.

But in 2016 people started coming out in record numbers to vote in some of the primaries. Long lines were common in some areas and early on some voting locations ran out of ballots. This was something that was not expected and some polling places were not equipped to handle the much larger than expected crowds.

Many people think that Trump was responsible for this record turnout and of course Trump took credit for it. But with this particular claim he might have some merit in taking the credit for the increased number of people coming into the Republican Party. At least it appears so when you look into things a bit.

For people to start coming out in record numbers after 2 elections that saw voter turnout decline, there has to be a reason for this change in voter apathy. Personally I think two factors played into this overall new level of engagement.

The first factor is that people were getting more and angrier over the years and that anger was sufficient to cast apathy to the sidelines and actually get people out there to vote. Judging by the voters who appear at rallies and campaign events this appears to be the case. People want change, they want it now and they are going to use their votes to get that change.

The second factor is that for the first time in several elections you have fringe candidates from outside the political system running in these primaries. In other words, the voters just didn't have to choose between a group of politicians, they had non-politicians out there they could vote for as well. They saw a real possibility for change and they latched on to it and exercised their right and civil duty to vote.

I think candidates like Trump and Ben Carson as well as other candidates such as Carly Fiorino gave the people hope that change cold actually happen instead of just being promised to them by politicians who once elected would just go back to supporting their own interests and the interests of the special interests.

I also think that is why Democratic Candidate Bernie Sanders captured so many votes as well. The primaries on the Democratic side turned out to be not quite the cake walk Hillary or the party expected.

This again was evidence that people did not want more of the dysfunctional government they have had for the last decade or so.

But one very interesting fact is that despite people wanting change and voting for new and different types of candidates, voter turnout on the Democratic side was not that much different from previous elections. At least not to the extent of the increases the Republicans were seeing.

So you need to ask yourself why you were seeing these huge increases on one side and not on the other. This is where Donald Trump's claim that it was primarily because of him starts to take on some real weight. You have to at least consider that Trump is the reason people started coming to the polls to vote.

But then you need to ask yourself why were they coming? Were they there to embrace Trump and his views and policies or were they coming out to vote for other candidates to keep Trump from winning? I am sure there were some people voting on either side but one thing was certain, voter turnout on the Republican side was been much higher than it was in the two previous elections.

I'll let you decide exactly why that's so. Regardless of the reason bringing new people into the voter booths is good for everyone and also for the Republican Party. Now all they have to do is sustain that growth and keep these new voters engaged in what is happening in this country.

I believe that overall the fact that some candidate, most probably Trump and a couple of others, are bringing new people into the party will breathe new life into what may have become a cynical and unresponsive system. I also think this is good because these new voters who are either in the party for the first time or have come back after a lengthy absence, will become more vocal and outspoken until things are changed to give them a bigger and louder voice.

As we have already or will discuss throughout this book if either party is to survive let alone grow they are going to have to bring new voter in and be more responsive to their needs. The very fact that both parties find themselves in awkward or embarrassing positions this election is because they have become so disconnect with the general public.

This has also come from the fact that up until this year no one had had the nerve or desire to challenge the status quo. But now challenges are being made, people are being made aware of things they never thought existed or happened and questions are being asked.

In this case I believe that Americans have won in that there are bound to be changes made that will benefit the people and make their votes more important.

Since this was one of the reasons for Trump running for President one can make a strong argument that he has helped start this debate and has not allowed it to be swept under the table as it has been for so many years.

The Art of the Deal

For those of you that might not know, Trump authored a book several years ago titled "The Art of the Deal". This bought was an accounting of how people can create and close out very good deals both in business and sometimes in their personal lives as well. It involved the use of certain techniques and processes designed to get optimum results.

As I started watching the debates I became interested in them not just for the information I got out of them but also to look at how the various candidates conducted themselves during the debates. This turned out to be the most interesting part of the debates for me.

It dawned on me around the third or fourth debate that several of the candidates, including Trump, were methodical in their approach each one concentrating on getting another out of the race. Trump went after Carly Fiorino while Marco and Ted went after Christ Christie and Rand Paul. Sometimes candidates banded together to attack just one other candidate at the time.

All of this was done in such a way that it dawned on me that this was exactly how business deals were won and lost and it was not lost on me that Trump has made a very nice living making deals and getting things done. So I started paying close attention to what was happening and how it could related to winning a competition such as a debate and creating and closing a deal out in the business world.

Trump started out making his presence known which was extremely difficult for many of the other candidates. While Trump dominated both the stage by being center stage for every debate or by being the focus of several of the questions, he soon positioned himself as the primary focal point of the debates. Ted Cruz and Marco Rubio begin on either side of Trump and did the same.

On the other side candidates like Chris Christie, Rand Paul, John Kasich and Carly Fiorino quickly found themselves getting less and less airtime and exposure. This did not happen by accident as Trump, Cruz and Rubio also made certain their names and faces were constantly seen on the news programs as well. This became such an issue that at one of the debates John Kasich sarcastically thanked the moderator for finally sending a question his way.

It is also not an accident that the candidates who established themselves in the media to the strongest extent were also the ones who dominated the debates as well.

Trump made controversial comments and Rubio and Cruz were the first to call out those comments and feign mock outrage. All the while the other 8-9 candidates were relegated to the second class debate or page 5 in the newspapers. Trump and Cruz were on page one, everyone else was several pages back.

But throughout the process Trump has followed a specific plan of attack that has worked extremely well for him up to the present day. A plan that is not necessarily a political plan but an effective business plan as well. Not obvious to many unless you really dissected it over time but still effective.

Trump set his sights on a few candidates that were not strong in the first place and those candidates soon left. Rand Paul and Carly Fiorino couldn't stand toe to toe with Trump and Cruz. But Trump also allowed the other candidates to do most of the attacks on the other candidates while he primarily concentrated on Cruz and Rubio who he rightly thought of as his primary competition. In other words, he stood by as others were eliminated from the ranks.

It was also interesting to watch other candidates attack Trump using various strategies that mostly backfired. It seemed that whoever tried to attack Trump was the next one to go.

Attacks made other appear weaker while either not denting Trumps image with his supporters and in some cases making them stronger and more dedicated. I liken the entire process as a kind of political chess game between the candidates. They were all jockeying for position and planning their next moves moving forward.

Another interesting fact was that these debates were not only commanded by Trump but they also produced sound bites and media coverage of some of the exchanges that further placed Trumps name in the papers and his face on the television screens. Every outrageous comment or controversial remark meant more news coverage and more free media. In one network it was estimated that Trump received 3-4 times more coverage than any other candidate.

I am sure that this was not by accident. I am sure that Trump had his plan marked out well in advance and that he created his candidacy in much the same way that he creates one of his deals or as he designs one of his marketing programs. This is relevant because that is exactly what the primary system is designed to be. One giant and national marketing plan to capture the nomination.

I watched him as the pool of candidates slowly dwindled to just 3 and even as one of those three no longer could get enough delegates to win.

I watched him change his tone and his approach over time to reflect the new conditions and the new goals ahead of him. I also saw him make mistakes and take missteps along the way as well.

But I also saw another side of his performance that perhaps was the most effective part of the whole persona. I saw his ability to take others off their message and to make their campaign more about Trump than it was about the issues. And the overall effect was and continues to be genius.

As things got more and more important and as the candidate list got smaller and smaller, Trump used other tactics that both entertained the voters while marginalized his opponents.

He referred to Marco Rubio as "Little Marco" which made it very difficult to see Rubio as a serious candidate when he was associated with that nick name. It wasn't a nasty nick name but it accomplished its objective and that was weakening Rubio's stature among the candidates.

And then we have the nick name for Ted Cruz "Lyin' Ted" because of the way he either lied or bent and twisted the truth. This name in particular resonated with the people who openly chanted it in rallies and other events. Not only was this a negative nick name but it called into question that overall character and trustworthiness of Ted Cruz.

These might be all little things that you might not think have much effect on a candidate but it is little things like this that can change the way voters perceive other candidates. They also produce amazing sound bites and increased air time and the public really seemed to like them.

Over time I saw more and more of the debates focused on Trump related questions and Trump related issues. I also noticed that the other candidates were talking about Trump in their answers and at their rallies and other events as well. In some cases they were talking more about Trump and his candidacy than they were talking about their own.

When it comes to marketing a product or service, or in this case a political candidate, the idea is to create brand recognition and that means how well others know about you and your product and how engrained it becomes in the media and with the people. But having other candidates and the media covering every comment and every rally, Trump has achieved what most politicians openly covet.

Free exposure, free airtime and the help of the competition in building their own personal brand. Every time someone hears your name or sees you on television their perception changes. You begin to establish relationships with people through the media and by using and crafting your words and responses carefully you can create a powerful perception in the minds of your viewers.

But the thing with Trump was that he did not play that game. He said what was on his mind even if it was offensive to some and outright mean to others. But if he felt it he said it and that was what captured the votes of so many Americans. He wasn't playing the role of a candidate. He was playing the role of an everyday person and utilizing a marketing plan to capitalize on that persona. And is did and continues to work for him very well.

While some people might say this is all an act or an accident, I truly believe that this entire persona and campaign has been carefully crafted every step of the way. Sure there were mistakes and missteps along the path but Trump has navigated through a system he really doesn't know that well and he has emerged as the front-runner.

That's good marketing for you.

What is Wrong with "America First?"

Recently I watched a Trump speech on foreign policy. I honestly have to admit that it was a bit light on details and specifics but in some cases that is more the norm at this stage of the campaign regardless of who is making the speech. But the overall tone of the speech for both foreign and domestic decisions was that he would be placing America first and other second when he made decisions.

This was roundly booed by his opponents and cause concern overseas with other countries and their government. Though the overseas reactions were to be expected because they had much more to lose once we started putting ourselves first, the reactions of Cruz and other political figures was a bit puzzling. At least to me.

I do not feel that it is wrong to put our interests ahead of other countries. We should be making decisions based not just on the needs of others but according to our needs as well.

If something doesn't make sense from our point of view then perhaps we maybe, just maybe, should think twice about doing something just because someone else needs us to.

I am not saying we should spend all our money in our own country. I am not an isolationist and I believe that we must continue to play our own role in the world governmental system. We have a responsibility as one of, if not the most, powerful nation in the world. But that responsibility should not be so great that we can no longer protect our best interests and the interests of our own people.

People are upset because we send billions and billions overseas to help other countries and their people while homeless in our country is a huge problem. People are frustrated because we help countries take care of their needs while we don't have the money or the same commitment to take care of our veterans many of whom come home with physical or psychological issues or both.

People become frustrated when companies move their facilities and operations overseas taking with them all their jobs while they make themselves rich at the expense of the American people. All because our tax laws and other laws allow them to do so without penalty or tariffs.

Then there are the various trade deals and deals we make with other countries that strongly favor the other countries at the expense of our own. We don't even get the same treatment in other countries as we give their products in our country. People like me wonder why that is and why those deals were made in the first place.

I do not believe that we should have to take a back seat to any country just because we are big and powerful. I believe that a strong America plays a vital role in the world we have today and we must again become strong so that what we say and what we do has meaning once again.

When you deal from weakness you become vulnerable. Schoolyard bullies pick on the weakest and strongest because they are not afraid of them. The same goes for America. If they perceive us as weak they will become bolder and more aggressive because there is little to fear. But if we become string and powerful again and use that strength and power properly, the entire world will become a more stable and safe place to live.

But it appears that society now feels that looking after your own interests first is somehow ethically wrong and socially irresponsible. While I am not one of those people who thinks that we should take care of ourselves and forget about everyone else, I do believe we need to re-evaluate what we do at home in relation to the rest of the world.

I liken our support of the rest of the world to business in many ways. But the underlying principle when it comes to business is that you make decisions based on the overall health and company interests as well as the interest of the customer. In other words, you cannot always give the customer what they want or ask for if it is to the detriment of the company.

The rationale for this approach is that if you make all your decisions based on others you place the future of the company at risk. If the company should fail or go out of business then it is not there to help anyone. The same principle should apply to our role in the rest of the world.

Other countries act as if we have a responsibility to resolve the world's problems and that we should offer unlimited funds in order to accomplish that goal. They see us as someone who should step in to take care of issues when at times the countries involved in those issues either resist our help or don't try to help themselves. So I agree with candidates who claim we cannot continue to play this role to the extent that we are playing it.

I agree with Trump when he says that other countries need to pay their fair share in relations to what is expected of America.

I also do not think it is right when we have such a huge deficit and cannot take care of our own infrastructure that we should be rebuilding the infrastructure of another country. Granted there are exceptions when it comes to disasters or other situations but we must stop the hemorrhaging of money going out of the country and start rebuilding our own country.

There is nothing wrong with putting America's needs and priorities first. This should not be considered selfish or as isolationism. Instead it should be seen in much the same way as a family budgeting their dollars and a business helping to insure that its long and short term future is being protected.

As one might understand, governments and people overseas are not happy with this approach and neither are American citizens with family or friends in those countries. And then we have the idealists and protesters who think it is our responsibility to give everyone what they need whenever they need it.

I do not think that anything should be taken off the table when it comes to taking care of other people and other countries. But we should not be expected to pay the lion's share of the expenses when there are other countries with plenty of money to contribute as well. As with everything in life things should be negotiable and out interests should always be front and center.

All too often we are taken advantage of by countries and governments that we are afraid to stand up to for some reason. While I am by no means a political expert, and while I realize we have a responsibility to the world to be a stabilizing and strong partner, I do believe we have to restructure the system to be fairer to us and all the other countries.

But this is a political hot potato with our candidates pandering to the voters in certain areas and tailoring their words and positions to suit their audience. And when Trump says that America should not be paying 3-4 times more than other countries and that some countries are paying nothing at all of a mere fraction of what they committed to pay, his opponents are indignant and clash with Trump.

The fact remains that we have a huge deficit that costs us more and more in interest payments every single day. Interest payments that take our tax dollars and get us nothing in return. This is something that needs to be addressed and we need a President who is ready, willing and able to take this matter on head-on and straighten it out. Someone who will not be bullied on the world stage or be more concerned about getting things fixed than political correctness.

Rubio Downfall

One of the most interesting aspects of this Republican election was the candidacy of Marco Rubio and his involvement with both Ted Cruz and Donald Trump. As someone who enjoys watching and evaluating interpersonal reactions such as these, this was one for the ages and a classic example of one person overwhelming another and causing that person to change their approach or reactions.

Early on in the elections Rubio had developed a reputation as being the future of the Republican Party. Blessed with good looks and a more than passable public speaking ability he was forecasted to accomplish great things. Of all the candidates running at the start, it would not have surprised me had the party anointed him the party favorite? Possibly alongside of Jeb Bush because of the family heritage in play there.

But as the debates went by Marco became frustrated with Trump's continuing popularity and his growing support.

He often fell into second or third place in the debates and although he had good ideas and a good working knowledge of how government worked, he simply could not push through part Cruz and Trump. But it was Trump who constantly bested him at least according to the media.

Trump started referring to him as "Little Marco" making him appear smaller in stature and not as strong as a Presidential candidate needs to be and that nick name had to frustrate him as well. Over the course of a few debates he tried asserting himself and speaking about the issues but still coming in second or third best especially behind Trump.

I'm not exactly sure who came up with his approach or plan of action but he soon became more about fighting Trump than expressing the issues. He and Cruz began an almost constant assault from either side on Trump and at times Trump didn't know what to do so he fought back in the way that Trump knows all too well. He fought back with nick names and rhetoric. But it was rhetoric with a slice of truth behind it.

It was long known that Rubio had the worst voting attendance record of all Senators and Trump called him on that as well as the fact that Trump was leading Rubio in Rubio's own home state of Florida where Trump was a part-time resident. Perhaps it was the frustration or the fear of losing his home state but Marco then made what would soon become known as one of the worst decisions ever made by a political candidate.

He tried to out trump Trump.

He abandoned his approach, the approach that had gotten him this far and instead adopted a negative and abusive approach where he interrupted and poked fun at Trump and did his very best to discredit him in bizarre ways like making fun of his hands and other loony things. He tried to get into Trump's head.

But the reality was that it was Trump who got into Rubio's head and caused him to abandon what had been successful for him so far. The result was that the voters saw someone turn into something he was not just to win a few votes. They saw a phony who was trying to be someone other than himself and it cost him dearly.

His numbers tanked, his family told him they didn't like what he had become and he tried to change back to what we was but the damage had been done. With his state's primary just around the corner there was not time for him to rehabilitate his image and his apologies were too little too late.

Ted Cruz didn't have to do a thing except watch Trump and Rubio go at it because whomever lost would mean one of Ted's chief rivals would either be very weakened or totally out of the race. So he just stood by, made a comment every so often to stick the knife in further and he let the process take its course.

What Trump was able to do was lead Rubio, who should have known better, away from his strengths and his message and get him to play the Trump game which he was ill-equipped to play. It just was not within his personality to be that type of person. He allowed himself to be played and it was shocking to me that no one in his campaign told him this was a very, very, very bad idea.

So the vote for Florida came in and Trump not only won but he beat Marco very badly in his home state and he captured all of the state's delegates. This was a huge blow to Marco and the Republican Party because he was the poster boy for the future of the party.

Rubio had no choice soon after but to drop out of the race seeing that he did not have the level of support that he needed to continue. He dropped out leaving just the core of three candidates of Trump, Cruz and Kasich.

The future of the party would have to be rehabilitated and rebuilt. He not only wasn't a candidate anymore he was no longer a Senator either having left that post to concentrate on his Presidential campaign.

This was a classic example of getting into the head of another person and getting them to do things out of frustration or desperation. Most of the time this takes the person out of their strengths and places themselves at a disadvantage when dealing with others. It is all about gaining the advantage in the process as early as possible and waiting for someone to make a mistake and then capitalizing on it.

This was a shame because I actually liked Marco Rubio although I thought he was a bit too young and unseasoned to make a good President. I think his time has yet to come and I think he has learned some valuable lessons this year throughout his first bid. I don't think he will make the same mistakes again nor do I think he will underestimate any future opponent either.

I also think that if Marco can get back into the political arena and pick up more experience and develop more accomplishments he will develop more self-confidence along the way as well. He was a far better choice than many of the other original 17 candidates but he just didn't have what it takes to come out on top this year. He has the looks and the personality to go far if he just sticks to his ideas and principles.

But what happened to Marco is a classic example of what happens to people when they are taken off message or when they lose focus. This applies not only in politics but in life as well. Whenever you try to become someone you are not bad things happen.

Just ask Marco Rubio.

Cruz Control

When I first started watching the debates I admittedly did so because of Donald Trump. Like many people I was curious as to how he would perform, what he would say and how he would hold up against career politicians with a ton of name recognition. At the same time I was interested in some of the other candidates as well but mostly Trump.

I had heard of Ted Cruz and I readily admit I had a negative opinion of him from the start based on some of the things he did as an early member of the tea party and how he was perceived in the Senate.

I am a strong believer that how people think about someone is usually a pretty good indicator regarding the type of person someone really is. This is especially true when it comes to people who see you day in and day out and at your best and when you are at your worst.

In Ted's case, it has widely been stated that almost no one likes Ted or thinks highly of him in the Senate. In fact, one of his fellow senators openly stated that if Ted were shot on the Senate floor with all the doors locked you would never get a conviction! Nice words for a co-worker, right?

But I also think that everyone should make up their own mind and use other things as input or data helping to come up with their own perception of someone. We are all different and not everyone likes everyone else. For me, these debates were a chance for me to see first-hand what type of person Ted Cruz really was.

From the beginning there were things that I didn't like and a few things that scared me a bit about Mr. Cruz. The first thing was something that Marco Rubio and a few other candidates did as well and that is telling the audience how you came from parents who came over with nothing but a dream and how they worked 14 menial jobs to support their family and now they have a son running for the President of the United States.

While the stories may very well been true they also were probably embellished but also were delivered with a kind of insincerity that to me was very obvious. They were told to tug at the heart strings of certain people and to develop an image of fighting for the weak and down trodden. I also find that when these stories are told over and over again during several debates that there is a reason for that and it is not to salute their parents for a job well done.

But what disturbed me even more than that was how many candidates would twist the words of what another candidate said to make it mean something totally different all by claiming they were upstanding, totally honest, religious people. No one did that more or better than Ted Cruz and it annoyed the hell out of me.

One such example was when the issue of Planned Parenthood came up. All the candidates blasted Planned Parenthood for performing abortions and a few other things. Ted called for Planned Parenthood to be shut down as did a few other candidates. But Donald Trump pointed out that they also provided other critical services for women and that the agency should not do abortions anymore but should still provide these valuable services to women. In some cases Planned Parenthood might be the only source of these services for the women that needed them.

Now Ted saw this differently and instead of giving the entire quote he condensed it down to "Trump Supports Planned Parenthood!" Ted is famous for this kind of stuff and sometimes it makes my head explode.

I also realize that spinning issues to fit a candidate's agenda is part of the political game and I have no problem with that. But you have to have a certain amount of straight talking and credibility to do that. As far as I can see so far after what, 13 debates, he is more interested in making someone else look bad than he is about telling the truth.

His positions usually are formulated so that he is vehemently against whatever someone else says. Not just Trump but the other earlier candidates as well. Lately it seems that Cruz is the latest person that Donald Trump has entered the mind of. He simply cannot answer a question without mentioning Trump.

Here is an example of ow even the simplest question might be answered by Ted Cruz:

Moderator: "Today scientists at Cal Tech, after careful and intensive research concluded that the sky is blue. How do each of you respond to this revelation? Mr. Trump, I will start with you."

Trump: "Well Anderson, this morning when I woke up and looked outside it was dark because I like to get an early start on the day as you well know. But as the sun came up it revealed a beautiful blue sky so I would agree. But that sky will only stay blue as long as we protect our planet."

Moderator: "How about you, Mr. Cruz?"

Cruz: "Well, Anderson, that is a very interesting questions and I think you for asking it. Of, course if you are a billionaire living in a luxury high rise building in New York your sky is going to be blue. But what about the millions of middle and lower class people struggling to make ends meet? Is their sky really blue?

My parents were immigrants with just a dream in their hearts when they came over to this fine country and they each worked 14 jobs to give their children a chance at the American dream. I'm sure they worked so hard they never had time to see what color their sky was. But their son is now on the stage to become the next President of the United States and that's what living in this great country is all about. And Andersen, I will not rest until each and every American, not just the Trumps and other one percenters of the world, have their own blue sky. I say to everyone out there listening that if you are tired of the Trumps in the world keeping their nice blue sky all for themselves then join us as we fight for the rights of everyone. Grab your own piece of blue sky by going to tedcruz.org and joining our team by making your own tax deductible contribution. That's tedcruz.org."

Most recently one well-known talk show host became so frustrated with Ted that he stopped him mid answer and told him to stop avoiding the question and to answer it. When Cruz got nasty and told him he would if he weren't interrupted the talk show host replied that Cruz does this all the time and he was sick of it. He wanted a straight answer to a specific question without the spin and without avoiding the question.

I think that pretty much sums it up.

Cruz also loves to hold himself up to different standards than other candidates. When Kasich was mathematically eliminated he said Kasich should quit the race. When he was eliminated he scoffed at such an idea. One set of values for him and another set for everyone else.

He states openly that Trump cannot win because 62% of the American voters did not vote for Trump. Then he goes on to say that he has won the last 5 elections. Like the two are directly comparable. The facts really are that even though 62% of voters did not vote for Trump he still had 2-3,000,000 more votes than Cruz which means that far less than 38% of all voters voted for Cruz.

Cruz loves to compare different things in order to make him look better in comparison. He will not compare apples to apples so to speak because that doesn't work for him. It's like someone asking you what your favorite color is and you answer is: 12. It just makes no sense to compare different things like they have a direct correlation between them.

Early on he tried to paint Trump as a phony because he gave contributions to the Democrats when he was running his business. This is something all businessmen do to keep on the good side of the politicians.

It was nothing earth shattering or unusual. He tried the "guilt by association" route but really got nowhere with it because the people saw through it or just didn't care.

I think what really has bothered me from day one about Ted is that he seems to have no limit on what he will do in order to get a vote. He cheated Ben Carson early in the race telling his voters that Ben had left the race. He then sent out misleading voter ballots to frighten people into voting for him. And there seems to be no fact he will not twist or spin and no limits to what he will say to create his desired position.

I know I have said this before but it is something that I believe the people are finally seeing about Ted Cruz. If you make an allegation there has to be some kind of real fact at the base of that allegation. You cannot take something, create an evil component to it and sell it to people as the truth. It just shouldn't work like that. Yet apparently it does.

People either like or hate the Lyin' Ted moniker and some might say it is disrespectful. But there is more than a thread of truth behind the nickname and Cruz himself has not responded to the challenge. He just plays it off by stating that "Donald loves to call people names" as if there is no truth behind it.

But if you tell people lies like another candidate has left the race so vote for him instead or you spin everything into something you can use to discredit another candidate and when you have a different set of standards and values for yourself and some other values for everyone else, that's a problem.

But casting all of this aside, let me tell you the thing that really bothers me about Ted Cruz. For Ted it is not enough that he lives his life according to his values. Instead he demands that everyone live by his values. If he is against something then everyone needs to be against it. If he believes something is right, everyone should believe it is right. If he believes something is wrong, everyone should believe it is wrong.

There is no mid ground. You are either with Ted or against Ted. And if you are against Ted you are wrong. If you vote against Ted in the Senate, you are wrong. If there is a bill up for vote in the Senate and there is something Ted doesn't like about it he will not just vote NO he will fight to squash it by any means necessary.

While some might think it is laudable to stand up for what you believe in, always being inflexible and having to get everything you want to nothing at all happens is one of the primary reasons why we have government grid-lock today.

People need to see this and understand this and I believe they are close to doing so if they haven't reached that point already.

Think about it for a while and you will see that I'm right.

Super PACS

Campaign financing rules were changed to limit the amount of money that any individual, company, organization or union could donate to any political candidate. While the intent of these PACS was good in that they made it illegal for anyone to donate huge amounts of money and therefore have considerable influence over a candidate, as usual people found ways around the system so that they could accomplish exactly the same thing perhaps even worse.

Technically Super PACS (Political Action Committees) are not controlled by the candidate and they cannot contribute or provide money directly to the candidates either. This is designed to retain the integrity of the campaign finance system although it really doesn't accomplish that goal at all.

For example, let's say a powerful union wants to get a favorable law or ruling from the government. In the "old days" they would send millions of dollars to the candidate with the intent being to get their vote on that ruling or other matter.

Now there are limits as to how much anyone can donate or give to a campaign so instead that union donates to a Super PAC and that PAC then pays for television advertising and other expenses on an independent basis.

Can everyone see the potential problems with this system? Of course you can but it gets worse. Of course it does.

When a candidate creates their ad or commercial they have to put in a statement saying that they approved this message. We have all seen or heard that spoken at the beginning or end of the ad. This is to make sure the candidate says they were aware of the content of the message so they cannot claim ignorance later if something went wrong with the ad.

So if a campaign puts out an ad claiming that another candidate took bribes or had sex with barnyard animals the candidate would be held responsible both legally and in the eyes of the public. Again, this was done to increase the factual contacts of the ads and to keep defamation and other similar issues in check.

But an ad could be put out from a Super PAC that says exactly the same thing and the candidate is not mentioned in the ad, does not have to provide a disclaimer and is not held accountable or responsible for the content of the ad. The result is that obnoxious or inaccurate ads can be aired, paid for by the PAC and the candidate they benefit gets almost a free pass.

So far every candidate, even Trump who is financing his own campaign, has Super PACs loyal to their campaign. Jeb Bush leads the way with a Super PAC worth over $80,000,000. Cruz has over $20,000,000 in loyal Super PAC money while Trump had about $5,000,000. Of course these are only rough figures and can change at any given moment. The idea is to show you just how much money is in these PACS and how they can influence a campaign.

There is also another way these PAC's can be used and it is an interesting application. While most of the PAC's support a candidate or groups of candidates, this year we have seen other PAC's exist for the express purpose of opposing a candidate. That means the PAC does not support or endorse another candidate but just wants to harm a specific candidate.

For example, there are a few of these PAC's that openly state they are opposed to a Trump nomination and they use their money to fund anti-Trump messages in all types of media. Anti-Trump PACS have over $15,000,000 to spend on their ads and other endeavors.

Though these PAC's are not controlled directly by the candidates, it is extremely naïve to think that there is not some kind of communications between the campaigns and these Super PACs.

Remember that individuals, groups and organizations are contributing millions of dollars to these PAC's and they are not doing this out of the goodness of their hearts.

It's one of those systems designed basically for a good reason but has just made things worse in the process. Candidate can still have access to the money their campaigns need and even now have a layer of isolation between them and the individuals or groups that contribute to them. So the very system that was designed and placed into service to control this type of activity has in fact made it easier for people to donate large sums of money to advance the candidates they support.

We are a country that was built on individual rights and the freedom of speech so it is difficult to create a system that someone cannot possibly find a shortcut to beat the system. I normally do not like people who complain about something without at least having some idea of how to change it but I find myself in that position right now.

If you abolish these large contributions all together then someone is going to take this to court saying their rights to support a candidate running for office has been violated. If you have a campaign financing law that makes all campaign financing done by the government that does not stop these individual groups from creating these PACs either. So the answer is not a simple black and white answer.

But candidates can and do use these PAC's to create and display ads that they do not wish to be connected to. One classic example this year was the ad featuring a near nude picture of Trump's wife, Melania, with a caption asking if this is who you want to be your first lady. It came from a PAC, Cruz denied any knowledge of it and claimed he had nothing to do with it and his name was never spoken to seen in print in the ad.

I am not saying these ads are wrong or even inappropriate though some of them really are but what bothers me is that now candidates can use these PAC's and the money they provide to do certain things that they cannot be connected to by the public. This means candidates are free to distribute lies, mistruths and other messages and then stand back and claim ignorance or even come out against those same ads after they have done their damage.

While I understand that politics itself is a dirty business and that there are things that go on behind the scenes that are technically not illegal, I think the existence of these Super PAC's and how they are used is disturbing and in some cases keeps the public from understanding what is true or coming from the candidate and what is false or rumor coming from the PAC's with the blessing of the candidates.

This is also not a single candidate issue. All the candidates have these PAC's supporting them and they all have the same abilities to use them indirectly in ways they choose. In these cases we are relying on the values and morals of the candidates and those running the campaign to make the right judgments and run the right ads. Today that is expecting and asking an awful lot from a system that is rooted in questionable actions and practices.

Airtime

If you have a product to sell, you want to get it in front of as many people as possible. You want to expand your market share and get your product seen by as many people and as many times as possible. This is how you grow your brand and this is how you gain awareness with the people.

But media time, both in the [press and on television, is not cheap and political candidates have to raise a ton of money to pay for all the ads we see almost on a daily basis. It also takes multiple exposures of a message in order for it to register in people's minds so the ads you see must be run over and over in order to reach their desired purpose which is to change you perception of the candidate.

The Cruz campaign and other campaigns have benefitted by the Super PAC's that pay for some of these ads and other types of advertising.

But even if their PAC's, or other organizations money is paying for these spots, they still cost money. Money that might be able to be spent on additional or different resources instead. So no matter who pays for something it still costs the campaign something.

Unless you can find a way to get exposure for free instead of paying for it.

This is something that the Trump Campaign has managed to do better than anyone else and this has not happened by accident. His free exposure on new channels and news programs of all types has been far greater than any other candidate. And all of this exposure has no cost Trump a single penny.

Television news and newspapers and other media fulfill two primary purposes, they informs their readership and they entertain them as well. If they fail at either of these objectives they will lose the interest of their viewers or subscribers and that is a death knell for any media outlet.

First and foremost for his entire career Trump has been an excellent marketer and promoter. You do not get to where he is in life without being able to market and promote. You cannot even be a top drawer politician without these same skills either. But these are not skills that are taught in school or at the university. They are skills you learn by watching others and through the experiences you have in life.

Trump has some of the most valuable real estate holdings and buildings in the world. These are buildings and golf courses that are in locations coveted by many other builders. But they are owned by Trump and they were all made possible by the Trump brand that he has helped create for himself.

He is doing the exact same thing with his campaign. He knows how to entertain and he knows how to market and he understands how the media works. He can draw on his experiences with The Apprentice on Television. He can draw on his experiences as a businessman and public figure. Then he can use all of these experiences together to both inform and entertain the voters and the audiences.

Though it is a sad indictment on our society, people by and large want to be entertained as much as possible. Give people a choice between a boring new program that is 100% accurate but dull and a news program that gives you the information you want in an entertaining and sometimes amusing manner and most people will choose a little amusement over dull and boring.

You can say many things about Donald Trump and what he does and doesn't do but one thing no one can say about him is that he is boring. He understands the value behind a controversial sound bite and a contentious quote or interview. He understands what people and what the media wants and he gives it to him.

The news programs know that if they have him on that their viewers or readers will increase. They know that everyone is waiting to hear what he has to say next, who he is going to take on and who he might even ridicule or offend next. The more colorful and controversial the content, the more people that will come to see or hear it. That's just the way it works, like it or not.

Because of this, Trump has been almost a constant participant in all the Sunday morning political shows and almost every show on all the cable news stations. All of this exposure has enables Trump to get into the homes and in front of millions and millions of people and entertain them and hopefully provide them with a message that will resonate with them.

This is an important factor because no matter how amusing or shocking you might be if the message doesn't register with the people they might just laugh at the comments but vote for someone else. But that has not happened, at least so far, because his message has tapped into what a great deal of people are thinking.

So not only is his message entertaining and informative, it resonates with the viewers. They want more of Trump and they want to hear more about what he is saying and how he is saying it. They want to also see that they are not the only ones with the same feelings or beliefs. They want to hear someone say something without filtering it through a politically correct filter.

But the key of all of this is that by giving the media outlets and the people what they want Trump is getting hundreds of thousands, if not millions, of dollars' worth of free advertising. He is getting his message out to more people for far less money and this gives him an advantage in the marketplace. With him self-financing his own campaign this is even more important.

Ted Cruz is doing this as well with some of the statements he makes as well. He spins information to suit his platform and gets himself in front of people free in that way. But the interesting thing is that whenever he says something about Trump or another candidate, they look to that candidate for a response. When that candidate provides that response, they get even more free air time, newspaper space and they reach more people. And they do it all for free!

It is no secret that the front runner is almost always in the media to a greater extent simply because they are the front runner. No one cares what the #15th candidate thinks because it doesn't matter. But the number 1 or 2 candidate, people are about what they say, think and feel.

Just like an inventor likes to use a show like Shark Tank to get their product out in front of millions and millions of people at no cost, so do political candidates like to get free airtime to further their agenda. So it is not so much who is going to do it because they all do it.

It just all comes down to who knows how to do it best.

Taking Others off Message

We already touched this a little bit when we discussed the downfall of Marco Rubio but it really bares additional attention because this has played such a crucial role in this year's Republican Primary season.

Whenever an election or any other activity starts the people involved have a certain plan or agenda that they create that they feel will help them achieve their goal. They will determine how to best present themselves while detailing the weaknesses of others or their opponent so that they wind up victorious. This is not just a political strategy but also a strategy for most of what is competitive in life.

Most of the time if that strategy is well designed and thought out it will be as effective only as much as the candidate sticks to that strategy and is not distracted or confused throughout the process.

But whenever someone is taken off their strategy or starts delivering their message in a different way that is when trouble usually starts.

That is precisely why political debates are so valuable and useful in determining how well prepared each candidate really is to hold a particular office. It takes little effort to deliver a speech to a group of supporters where you have a captive audience that is supportive and not given the chance to ask questions or participate. But when you have a debate where other people can step in and change the approach or argue points right back at you that is something else.

Early on when there were far too many candidates people had to craft their answers in short segments while at the same time fighting for their share of time in front of the camera. That time was valuable and if candidates appeared confused or distracted or in any way intimidated, that was very bad for them and their future.

Trump excelled throughout the debates at taking others off message. What he managed to do with Marco Rubio was to not only take him off his message and instead start attacking Trump, he also made him abandon the personality that gave him his success to date in the process.

I think Marco has a future in politics and once he gets a little bit older and more experienced I think he will do fine as long as he has learned some lessons these past few months.

But the problems wasn't that his message or views was wrong. The problem was that he allowed another candidate, in this case Trump, to take him off message and cause him to become someone he wasn't.

Trump did this to other candidates as well and it did not work out well for any of them. Jeb Bush thought that taking on Trump was the right approach and it failed miserably. Even his family history and pedigree could not help him. Carly Fiorino found herself in the same position and she failed as well. Even Ted Cruz, the second place candidate did the same thing.

Ted Cruz, after finding himself behind by several hundred delegates, came off message as well. Not totally as he still tires to advance certain parts of his agenda and platform but if you look closely (even not so closely) you will see that every answer to every question mentions Trump. He is more concerned with making Trump look bad than he is about making himself look strong.

I don't think politicians give the people enough credit these days. They think that they can lie, spin, twist and abandon the facts as long as people don't realize what they are doing. But I think that a lot of people do know what they are doing and they are getting a bit tired of it.

How many times can someone hear that the third place candidate who is mathematically out of the race tell the people that he is the best candidate and in the strongest position to capture the nomination.

How many times can we listen to someone tell one candidate who was mathematically eliminated that he is just a spoiler and needs to get out of the race and then when he finds himself in the exact same position tell the people that he is one of two people with a clear cut path to the election?

People are funny in that they usually want to give people the benefit of the doubt especially at the beginning. They will except more at first value in the beginning and will either develop trust and accept more or develop distrust and accept less and question more moving forward.

When candidates go off message and start attacking other candidates instead of advancing their own positions and views eventually people will realize what they are doing. Most people do not respond well to that kind of activity unless they see truth behind it. But even when attacks are based in truth people do not want the candidates focus to be on attacks.

Attacks are fleeting and will end when the threat has been neutralized. Only then will the candidate return to his real message or agenda and by that time it might very well be too late.

You cannot turn on and off your ability to deliver an effective message because delivering an effective message is not a one-shot process.

Delivering a message should be directed at gaining the interest of new people while increasing the interest in people who already are following you. Interest builds with each exposure. The more positive experiences a voter has with a particular candidate the more likely it is that they will vote for them. Very few people make a decision based on a single comment or sound bite.

But the exact opposite can happen when someone hears something they don't like or they don't react positively with. In fact, a single negative experience can do far more damage to someone's perception than several positive experiences. So every time someone changes their message or alters the way they deliver that message it can cause problems within the campaign.

As I am writing this we are currently more than midway through the process with the Northeastern primaries a few days away. I watch Ted Cruz on the new channels and every other word out of his mouth is not about Ted and his campaign, his values or his positions on important issues. Instead, he concentrates on telling people how every other candidate is going to be a disaster and that is why they should vote for Ted Cruz.

Think about that for a moment. Whenever someone concentrates on telling you how bad someone else is and to keep them away they should vote for you, doesn't that show that you are having a hard time selling yourself on your own merits and instead have to make someone else look worse so that you look better?

The think that people don't realize all of this stuff but they do. And most candidates won't realize it until it is too late.

The Rigged System

One of the primary issues regarding the Democratic and Republican Primary system is the charge that they are rigged against certain candidates. Trump is the one making all these claims and I am not sure I agree with his choice of words but that doesn't mean that there is not something very wrong with the primary voting and delegate system.

I do not agree with Trump that the system is rigged against him per se as he claims. The fact is that the system is rampant with rules and abuses that could be used against any candidate given the right set of circumstances. In any case, both party systems are not wholly dependent or responsive to the people's vote no matter what the respective party heads might say or claim when they are interviewed.

I find it extremely interesting yet totally within character how the Republican Party head will just say over and over "The rules are the rules and the candidate know the rules." Or, my second favorite line which answers absolutely nothing: "This is the same system that elected Abraham Lincoln and we did all right there. If it was good enough for Lincoln it should be good enough now."

There are so many holes in those statements that they resemble Swiss cheese. So let's just discuss a few of the most glaring holes in these comments. I will leave it up to you to come up with any others that you might see because there are so many to choose from.

Society Changes

Like everything else in life society changes and people change along with it. Because of this systems, policies and other things that used to make sense or work well often no longer function as well as they used to. Think about the things in your life that are done differently or better now than they used to be done.

Because of this the argument that something worked just fine 100 years ago so it should work just fine right now just does not hold water or even make any sense. It is a flawed logic that just cannot be defended.

Technology Changes

Technology has changed at warp speed over the last 100 years. In fact it has changed dramatically in just the last 20 years. This enables us to do things that we never would have even contemplated 100 years ago. Technology has changed everyone's life over the years and you cannot escape that fact.

Today computers and other devices allow us to capture more votes in less time and to send that information to governments all over the country almost instantaneously. We no longer have to manually count votes or read voter machine and tally results. Everything is done by computer.

This means that some of the practices from earlier in time where logistics and distance helped create the policies and systems still in use today really no longer apply. We have the technology today to increase the meaning and weight of the individual vote and not isolate or minimize it like is often done today with the old system.

Longevity Does Not Mean it's Right

If you do something wrong, or use something that just doesn't work well for a long period of time that does not mean that it is good. It just means there are no other alternatives or that you are lazy for refusing to change or adapt what you do in life.

People seem to think that if something has been around for year it must be good. They feel this way about products they buy, brands they attach value to and other things in life that they are just accustomed to because they might not even realize that there are better alternatives out there. People dislike change and they dislike having to learn something new, do something differently than they are used to or apply the thought and effort to create something better.

The problem is unless the public demonstrates their dissatisfaction or someone takes the time and makes the effort to create change nothing will happen. Even when someone does come up with a better solution they still have to convince people to get out of their comfort zone and adapt to the current times.

On another level there is a nervousness about change and we all experience it. We feel that we might lose control whenever something changes or that something will be either taken away from us or reduced in some form if it changes. I am certain that the Republican Party realizes that its control over the so-called unbound delegates (more on that later) will go away if the system is changed to reflect the popular vote to a higher degree.

Glosses over Party Self-Interests

Whether you are a liberal or a conservative and regardless of the candidate you support or believe in, you have to realize that the system is at least partially in the control of the state and national Republican system. Voters do not vote for and elect every delegate that vote for their candidate of choice. There are always a group of other delegates who can vote across party lines for whomever they want regardless of who the voters voted for.

This, of course, is a huge advantage for the national party as they can influence these delegates to vote for the candidate that the party supports rather than the candidate the people support. If one candidate fights the interests of the party they can influence the unbound delegates to vote against that candidate. If there is a candidate the party loves, they can help assure that candidate the nomination by flooding them with these delegates.

While technically the party is not allowed to influence a delegate we all know that is can and does happen and there is no way to monitor this or protect the reliability of the system. Whenever you have a system that makes it easy to influence the outcome or result of something the more likely it will be that someone will use that influence to get what they want or need over the will of the people.

Minimize or Ignores the Vote of the People

Again, it doesn't matter which candidate you like or support. But you have to realize or at least understand that some of the states have rules or policies that just are not in line with the votes of the people in that state.

While some states have primaries that reflect the will of the people, some states have rules or policies that either make little sense or some that make absolutely no sense whatsoever. This is one of the reasons for the complaints of a rigged system.

A person example is the state of Pennsylvania where the votes of the people only count for about 15-16 of the state's delegates dedicated to that candidate that wins. The other delegates, even though they are elected by the votes of the people, can vote for any candidate they want to at the convention.

So, a candidate can get every single vote from the people but will have only a handful of delegates that they can count on. The other 50+ can vote for someone else even though the people overwhelmingly voted for someone else.

Now if that doesn't make sense to you, then let's take it one step further which is really bizarre.

The voters vote for particular delegates not candidates for [part of the ballot but the ballot lists only names of the delegates and not who they support. So unless you research each and every delegate to see which candidate they support you could wind up voting for someone else instead of your chosen candidate!

On the Democratic side they have something even worse and that is "super delegates". Now these delegates can leap over huge buildings in a single bound or bend steel in their bare hands but they are not elected by the people and can vote for ever the heck they want to! Hillary does not have an overwhelming lead in voter's delegates, but she has hundreds of these super delegates that make her lead as large as it is.

Now either party can argue until they are blue in the face but the fact is that both systems minimize the votes of certain people in certain areas and cede power back to the establishment or the party. Under this system the losing candidate could very well have a huge lead in the popular vote but these establishment delegates stack the system in the party's favor not the voters.

Claim of RNC Inability to Control States

Here is another thing that appears on the surface to make no sense.

The fact that the head of the RNC or DNC claim that they have no control over what the states do and how they run their state primaries. To expect the people to believe that the national committee, to which each state belongs, can go out and do whatever they feel like it whenever they feel like it is absurd. Even if that were somehow the case this would just be one more thing that needs to be changed.

You could look at this like a franchise business where each state is a franchise. In a franchise the franchisers all are bound by the rules of the company. While they are allowed a certain degree of latitude to compensate for local area differences, they are still bound by certain rules, policies and procedures. One of the benefits of a franchise system is uniformity and that is what the guidelines are in place for.

The party's would like for us to believe that each state is free to do whatever they want even if that eliminates the voters themselves. It appears this might be the case when it comes to certain states or they party likes this because they have more flexibility and options when it comes to picking their chosen candidate over the will of the people.

I am not saying that every state use exactly the same system, which would be nice, but they should have rules that are fair to the voters and all the candidates and not overly favorable to the party or establishment.

Rule Changes before Convention

OK, we have covered a lot about the system and hopefully most of you will agree with most of the comments and views on these pages. If not hopefully you agree with at least a few of them. But before we move on to the next chapter, let's discuss another truly bizarre rule of the Republican Primary system. This one might make you wake up and realize that something is truly wrong here.

At the beginning of the election cycle, candidates cast their hat into the ring and register as a Presidential candidate. When they register they are given a complete set of rules including what it takes to win, how to go about navigating each individual states system and any other pertinent information that the candidates need to know. Candidates then use these rules to help their campaign accomplish the goal of winning the nomination.

But then the delegates and a rules committee get together before the convention to see if any of those rules need to be changed. That's right, they look BEFORE the convention to see if any rules need to be changed! So the rules that every candidate has played by throughout the campaign now could mean little or nothing when they hit the convention.

Now, I am not saying that this could happen even though it has happened in the past but they could change a rule or two to increase or improve the chances of a specific candidate to capture the nomination. They could change the rules to make it easier to get their own candidate in or keep another candidate out. All after the primary system has run its course.

In summary, I am not sure "rigged" is the right word to describe how this system really is. It is rigged only when the party wants it to be as there are enough loopholes and party controlled aspects of the system to make it easy to influence the final results. But despite this the main problem I have is that this system is unfair for the voters.

So I guess "unfair" is a better word than rigged when it comes to the voters. For me I would love to see the candidate that garners the most votes become the nominee. I would like to see all the unbound or super delegates be retired and have the people decide who ultimately represents them.

Because this is not a Republican or Democratic issue. It is a voter issue and the people who pay their taxes and vote in the elections should have their votes matter. This should not be a system where the party tells the voters what's good for them. The people should decide that on their own with their votes.

Strategic Fighting
Collusion & Confusion

For those of you as old as I am you might remember an old classic TV show called "The Twilight Zone". This was a weekly show where weird and strange stories were told. There was nothing normal about the show or the stories and everything seemed to have a strange or unexpected twist at the end.

For the last month or so I have been hearing all the candidate sniping at one another but it always seemed like Ted Cruz was really sniping at John Kasich and these were not veiled or disguised comments but very obvious and pointed comments. He would tell Kasich that he should drop out of the race, that he had no chance of winning and that he was just a spoiler in the race.

Then it escalated to the point where Kasich fired back at Cruz and Cruz called Kasich "incorrigible" and it went downhill from there. Both of them were constantly at each other's throats each saying nasty things about each other in response to the last barb or insult.

But then this past weekend these two candidates who were constantly fighting and insulting each other decided to force a sort of alliance in order to slow down the momentum of Donald Trump. This was a twist that no one, including myself saw coming. It was the twist at the end of the "Twilight Zone" zone story.

The reasons behind this alliance were given as a "reallocation of resources" meaning that conceding certain states to certain candidates would allow both candidates to conserve resources and allow them to campaign heavier in certain areas in order to beat Trump. On the surface one might think that this makes sense but there are so many holes in this arrangement that one really has to wonder why it was put into place in the first place.

The rumor has it that Kasich was running out of money which appears to make sense since he has almost no chance of getting the nomination even at a contested convention. He just has too many delegates to sway or convince in order to reach the majority. The only possibility and saving grace for him might be that so many delegates have problems with Cruz and Trump that they might see Kasich as the best choice.

But even that is optimistic because if he somehow did get the nomination the voting public, seeing their votes disregarded would revolt and cause the destruction of the party. But then again, the party hasn't respected the vote of the people for so long and has become so arrogant it might not care or realize this.

Still, if the reason is money then perhaps this does make sense for Kasich because he really has nothing much to lose. He might even be angling, despite his protests to the contrary for a position in the Cruz administration. But with their difference and animosity between them this appears unlikely as well. But stranger things have happened.

On the Cruz side this is a real gutsy move as it has more downsides than potential upsides. It appears that Cruz is not lacking for money at this point and there are people who agree that should this go to a contested convention that he will wind up the winner on the second or third ballot. Whether or not this is true only time will tell.

If the alliance should result in more votes being cast for Cruz in some areas and Kasich in others then it could reduce the number of votes and delegates for Trump and make it harder for him to get to 1,237.

So anything that anyone can do to stop that from happening would be beneficial for Cruz because once Trump makes it to 1,237 it is over for both Cruz and Kasich.

The downside for Cruz is more substantial, however. If he keeps up his side of the bargain he has to rely on Kasich to get him votes in Indiana and for Kasich to make a strong showing in the states that Cruz concedes to Kasich. This might be high expectations for someone who has only won his home state. This might result in a big win, and more delegates for Trump.

Some people, myself included, feel that Cruz will take the reduced competition in Indiana after Kasich pulls out and then still campaign hard in the other states spinning it that this is the right thing for the country and screwing Kasich in the process. This is the kind of thing people expect Cruz to do but to violate the agreement in such a public and open manner could cost him delegates and support from his follower while also ruining his reputation within the party.

The other downside is that Kasich and Cruz supporters might not support the alliance as they are being told to. Many, if not most, people do not like to be told what they should do especially with something as personal as how they vote. Most of us vote on our principles and values and do not take kindly to people requesting we change our vote based on their interests and not the voters.

If the voters respond negatively, which they very well might since Cruz and Kasich do not share a lot of common ground in their campaigns, then the people must be upset that their candidate is violating their own principles and the result could be fewer votes for them and more for Trump. Or at least fewer votes for Cruz and Kasich if their supporters do not come out to vote as well.

There has been an almost universal opinion that this is a last ditch maneuver on both Cruz and Kasich's part because time and elections are winding down and little else has worked to stop Trump's momentum. It even has been said that the timing of this is strange as well as it would have made more sense to do it a month or so earlier to get the benefits for a longer period of time.

The other odd thing about this is that even though it was viewed as a significant, or even major move, neither candidate came out in strong support of it after the announcement was made. In fact, they appeared to play it down and even backtrack a bit by telling their voters that they should vote for them not the other. This appears to most as being contrary to what the alliance originally was supposed to be.

As all of this was going on Trump has seized on this opportunity to point out the weakness of both candidates and how both of them realized that they could not beat him one on one but instead had to collude with each other. (Wrong word to use but you get the gist of what Trump was saying.)

It is very interesting to watch these events transpire and notice which ones were well thought out and executed and which ones were botched almost from inception. This particular one was not only introduced at the wrong time but neither candidate would promote it and try to sell it to the people.

It was like the thought about it after the fact and realized that this was not a particularly good thing to have done. Then Cruz started spinning it, Kasich started rationalizing it and both candidates were not at all comfortable with discussing it. It doesn't sound like a very promising start to something that might have a significant impact moving forward.

Spin Cycle

I am a pretty tolerant person and can appreciate and even enjoy a good argument or discussion. I am not always right and I will admit when I am wrong but one thing I cannot stand is when someone tries to blow smoke at me and twist and turn the truth to support their agenda or viewpoints.

That being said, I have come to the quick decision that someone who feels like I do will not tolerate a debate or interview with a politician at all. Even the candidates you like can sometimes say things that make you scratch your head and wonder where the hell that got their information.

In the interest of once again being upfront about my support for Trump, I have to say that other candidates seem to be very well adept at bending or twisting the facts. Cruz has a PhD in this area and apparently so do his campaign spokespeople. This doesn't mean that everything Trump says is true.

Lord knows he has made his fair share or stupid or questionable statements but after the after he has always accepted the blame or clarified his answers. This is one area where Trump's lack of political skills are clearly evident. This is probably one reason why many of his supporters like him.

I should also state at this time that I can appreciate and value that everyone has their own opinions about certain things. After all individual opinions and the ability to express them represent one of the greatest things about this country. So I am not against one candidate telling me they would not send ground troops into a certain area for a certain reason while another candidate says that they will. Different opinions on the same subject are common.

What I do object to are campaigns who manufacture their own facts or distort something and misrepresent it to suit their needs. One perfect example I have is when the Cruz campaign tells the people that 60% of the Republican voters did not vote for Trump so it is clear he is not the people's choice. But they neglect to mention, and scoff at it when it is brought up, that 70% of the people did not vote for Cruz! When you mention that, they spin it differently.

Same facts but different standards for the candidate and their rivals.

Then we have Kasich who still insists today when he has less than 20% of the front runner's delegates, that he has a clear path to the nomination.

People say that someone else changed their position on something so that proves they are not committed to anything and cannot be trusted. Their values and honesty are challenged. But when they change their opinion or stand to favor the voters today they call it adapting. Same thing, different standards for different people.

I already mentioned the distortion on Trump and Planned Parenthood and a few other examples.

I am not the smartest person in the world or sometimes in the same room but I have a ton of common sense and I can usually spot BS and similar crap from a mile away. I do not like it when someone tries to tell me they don't think I am smart enough to see through their crap. I only wonder just how many people take things at face value without really thinking all that much about them.

For me personally, I would appreciate a campaign where people just stood up and tell people the truth. Even when it makes them look bad. I guess that is one thing I like about Trump. While I don't agree with a lot of what he says or how he says it, I do not get the impression that he spins a lot of what he says. He just speaks from the heart and what's on his mind.

You might not agree with him, but you have to appreciate what he says without the need to spin   it   for   his   own   good.

Exposing Flaws

This book is all about how Donald Trump and America have already won even though he has not become the nominee at the time this is being written. But being a winner is not always about winning or losing a certain contest but instead by what you managed to accomplish along the way.

Sometimes the person who wins is not always the person who makes the largest long term contributions or makes the largest difference. Sometimes it is the person who tries the hardest and has other goals which might not enable him to win but to do more long term good.

In this election we have seen a few candidates, including Trump, who have not been shy about voicing their opinions and that is a very positive thing. But Trump at times has gone out of the way to make sure to point out certain things that usually are not discussed or even made public.

Though he is at time abrasive you most of the time can see the truth behind his message and you have to admire his willingness to say what others remain silent about. I am not going to get into policy discussions at this pint but instead will keep my thoughts and comments to the political system instead.

Call it ignorance or just being uninformed but I have learned more about our election system this year than I ever knew about it before. Not because the newspapers or television shows saw fit to enlighten the public about it but because Donald Trump and other non-political candidates were not afraid to speak out.

This is where Americas wins.

Just because something exists does not mean that it is fair and equitable to the public. As we have discussed and explained in several parts of this book, there are aspects of the system that take the general population and their votes out of the equation and substitute party chosen delegates.

While this has always existed it existed as kind of a foot note. In other words people sort of knew about this or casually might have heard about it but they never really knew just how much of this kind of stuff went on during an election.

They never heard about it because it was not in the best interests of the candidates or the party to have this kind of information made public. While the party claims this was all done transparently, the reality was the transparent parts were buried pretty deep for most of us to see.

Candidates did not talk about it even when the system worked against them because to do so would place their future with the party and the system in jeopardy. It was in their best interest to play along with the rules and take one for the team in exchange for support and help in the next election. This is how the system works now and how it has always worked.

Until this election.

This election had at least two main stream candidates, Donald Trump and Ben Carson (and to a far less extent, Carly Fiorino) who were not politicians and therefore were not concerned with having the party's help or assistance in future elections. They were in the race for this year and if they lost were hardly interested in running again in the near future.

The non-political candidates also were at least partially immune to the special interests as well especially Trump who was self-funding his own campaign. But it is unlikely that the big oil companies and big Pharma were spending a ton of money on Carson or even Fiorino. So there was another way they were at least mostly immune to being forced to accept the status quo.

The result of this was candidates who were quick to point out inequities and short comings in a system that most people thought was at least mostly fair. People do not expect perfection but they demand something close or at least something that tries to be fair. The current system accomplishes neither.

But candidates this year are not just pointing these things out to the public they are doing so forcefully and in Trump's particular case, very aggressively and making it part of his candidacy and overall campaign strategy. So this year we are seeing something totally different. We are seeing the gloves come off and the shortcomings of the system brought front and center and in the spotlight.

This has all been aided by the explosion of social media where people can now hear about things seconds after they happened instead of days or weeks like it used to be. Outrage is instantaneous now and no one can say or do anything under the radar anymore.

Popular candidates have millions of followers on Twitter and Facebook and other platforms and this gives them a way to contact every one of those personally and share the latest facts and developments. They can also send out links to certain information to further educate the voters and gain almost instant credibility.

Make no mistake about it, Social Media has played a huge role in bringing information out from the darkness into the living room.

The first step in changing something or making it better is to identify and understand all the flaws within the system. If you do not understand the flaws you cannot change them. When you fail to see the problems you never look for solutions. When you can bury something from view you can keep things quiet. But that is no longer possible.

Today you can see it on your smart phone, watch it on your tablet and find out up to the minute information on any of the 24 hours news channels. This is where people become aware and when change really starts. Nothing really stays quiet anymore. Someone always has a cell phone out to take a picture or record a video. Every single comments can be uploaded and played back almost instantly.

Some of this works in favor of the candidate and sometimes it backfires like when Trump published the unflattering picture of Mrs. Cruz. But the point is that this year candidates are not afraid to speak out and people like Trump have created a culture where it is not just all right to questions things and demand change but people are being encourage to do so.

It is far too early to see what all of this is going to lead up to but you can rest assured that some things will be changed because the public will demand it.

People will not be allowed to hide behind the status quo because others will see what they are doing. The more people speak out the better informed the rest of us become.

Just like I have learned more about our primary and election systems this year so have millions of others. And the more informed we become, the more we will facilitate change. Some people within the system may not like it and will openly and secretly resist it but if we continue to speak out changes will happen.

And that is why America has already won no matter what should happen from this day forward.

Change Worthy Behavior

One thing that I learned over the last few months is that there are problems within our election system. While that is not unusual in life there are things that can and should be changed. Easy things that do not require a massive overhaul or total redesign of the system.

The good thing about change is that we can usually make small changes that have a major impact for the better. Not massive changes but little tweaks that are needed to make things better or more efficient. But first we have to understand and identify exactly what needs to be changed.

There are many things that need to be changed about this year's election process both for this year and in the future. While I do not claim to profess the in-depth knowledge required to figure out everything that needs to be changed, here are the major things as I see them that need to change this year and moving forward:

Things that Need to Be Changed Now

Attitude

I really think we have to change the attitudes of the candidates to reflect a more refined and dignified process. This election was far too confrontational and at times juvenile in nature.

If Trump becomes the nominee he needs to tone down the insults a bit. While this is what helped him establish himself as a candidate in the first place we do not expect him to make radical changes but he needs to tone it down a bit. People are now calling it "acting more presidential" whatever that really means.

Cruz needs to stop or at least turn down the rhetoric and the constant anti-Trump and Kasich banter as well. It does not reflect well on him or his campaign and is probably hurting him in the polls as it is taking him off of message.

Both party's need to listen to the people more and stop the arrogant attitude that they are above and more important than the voters.

They need to be more responsive and make the will of the people more important than their own self interests. While I do not hold my breath waiting for this to happen the way they were blind-sided by the popularity of Trump just might open a few eyes within the party. The same for Sanders on the Democratic side. But don't count on it.

Honesty

Is it too much to ask to just be a bit more honest for the people? Can we stop filling the heads of the people with lies and distorted truths? From hearing Kasich still tout that he has a clear path to the nomination to Cruz telling us that he will win the most delegates elected by the people this has got to stop.

I would love to see the candidates answer the questions presented to them instead of advancing whatever agenda they have at the moment while evading the real answers. I would also like the media to be more aggressive in challenging the BS when they hear it and holding candidates and their spokespeople accountable.

I say that I would like to see this happen but I do not hold out much hope that it actually will. Politics is all about perception and candidates will always be twisting things around to make themselves look good while making their opponents look bad. It's just what they do.

But a bright spot this year is that during the last month it appears that some of the bigger or more popular shows are starting to challenge the candidates to start answering questions honestly. Cruz angered a journalist so much that he stopped the interview and told Cruz he was sick and tired of him evading answers. Other anchors have stopped him and told him to stop the anti-Trump rhetoric and just answer the questions. Other have openly challenged candidate's spokespeople as they tried to spin a story or sweep something under the table.

These are important advances in my opinion because they indicate a willingness to start challenging people in a more aggressive fashion. This, if it continues, will help us get more honesty from the candidates and the party leaders. Since this is how we get the information we need to make our decisions, this can only be better for all the American people.

Unbound Delegate Requirements

Unbound delegates are just not fair. They should be required to vote according to their state or districts voting patterns at least on the first ballot. The idea that a candidate could win the popular vote in a state in a landslide and still not get most of the delegates is not only unfair, it is disgraceful.

A simple rule change is all that is needed for this year and then the rules and systems can be changed over the next few years to make future elections more fair and more responsive to the will and votes of the people.

Things to Be Changed for Next Time & Beyond

Uniformity of Rules by State

This one just seems to make sense. Why should we have different rules for different states that are all in the same system for the same purpose? Whenever you change the rules by state you also change the value of the individual vote as well. So the vote case by someone in Wyoming might carry a totally different weight than the vote cast by someone from Pennsylvania.

All these different rules allow the party and the individual states to influence the results and help pick a candidate that may or may not be the candidate that the people want. Having a system that has this built in ability to be manipulated just makes it easier for people to abuse the system.

The only way to stop this is by making it harder for people to work around the system. Changing the system to make the rules and policies uniform across the board is the first step in this process.

Eliminate Unbound Delegates

Unbound delegates or for the Democrats, Super Delegates, need to be eliminated. The very idea that people can be assigned to vote for a specific candidate without the votes of the people is just unfair and reprehensible. You might as well tell the people that they are not intelligent enough to make the right choices so the party will see to it that the right candidate is nominated. Because that is exactly the message that is being sent to the people from both parties.

Have every delegate be obligated to vote for candidates based on the votes of the people. Stop having delegates waiting for the party and the special interests to tell them how to vote. At the most basic level, remove the ability or even the temptation to corrupt the will of the people.

Improve Value of the Individual Vote

I would love to see the average vote carry more weight. I would love to see the people elect the candidates and not the party or the establishment system. As it stands now there are too many ways for people to manipulate and even "fix" the system to choose a desired candidate. This would have happened this year had there been a [arty favorite candidate for the party to rally behind.

But this year people are scared of Trump but every in government can't stand Ted Cruz because of what he has done in the Senate. He has few supporters if any so there is no party favorite candidate to get behind and push through.

I like the fact that Trump, even though he has navigated the system well, continues to point out the unfairness and flaws in the system. I am sure he has an ulterior motive and that this approach makes it more difficult for back room deals to steal the nomination from him but it is just nice to have someone with the stage and the voice to bring these things out in the open.

Campaign Finance Reform

If you want to get completely rational about things, it makes no sense for people to spend 100's of millions of dollars to get a job that pays much, much less than that. But the amount of money to create and mobilize a campaign is enormous and contributions are one way that candidates get the funds to operate these campaigns.

But contributions are also a way for people to buy influence over candidates and this has been well known for a long time. This is not something that started with this election or even the last few elections. It has been going on for decades.

The last round of campaign financing reform was a start with limits placed on what people and businesses could donate to any candidate. But like any system people who really want to find a way around things usually can. So now instead of donating directly to the candidate and observing these limits, instead they donate to a Super PAC where they can donate pretty much what they please.

We need to have a system where the ability to buy influence and power is taken away from people and businesses. I am not sure what that system would be because we cannot take away the right to contribute for personal reasons. But we need to have more disclosure so everyone, not just the candidates, can see who contributed how much to certain Super and regular PAC's. This kind of transparency is really important if we are to seriously take out the contribution loopholes.

Make Super PAC's More Identifiable

Trying to reign in a Super PAC and how they operate is not going to be easy with people demanding their right to contribute money to their candidates of choice. Even though there are rules put in place to isolate the candidates from the day to day operation of these PAC's you would be foolish to believe that such a rule is never violated.

The communication might not come from the candidate him or herself but a mess delivered by a friend of a friend of someone's third cousin on his mother's side could easily provide instructions on what the PAC does on behalf of the candidate.

I have mentioned the shortcomings of this system several times in this book. But the most dangerous aspect of a PAC is that they get to put out whatever message they want and it cannot be traced back to the candidate or the campaign. The result can be slanderous, inappropriate and outright false ads that the candidate can let play for a few days and then come out against them after people have already seen them several times. Then everyone pleaded innocence and the damage has already begun.

I'm am fairly sure that we would not be able to eliminate these PAC's but to make them more transparent and to publish the names of the donors and the amounts that they give would be a great start. At least the people would them know who the message is really coming from since many of these are not tied to candidates.

The Media

Today the media plays a vital role in getting all kinds of information and news out to the public. The problem with some form of media is that the information they provide is either inaccurate to filtered to fit in with the particular views of that media source.

For example if a newspaper comes out in favor of one particular candidate their coverage of the candidate might be biased so they report only the good and omit the bad and vice versa for the other candidates. Because of this it can be difficult for people to get the right message delivered in a non-filtered or distorted manner.

Over the course of this primary process I have watched several different types of programs on many different networks so I could get not only an accurate portrayal of what was going on but also hear different sides of the issues as well.

Because this is the only way you can make intelligent decisions and proper judgments.

If I only watched Pro-Cruz shows or programs and read only Pro-Cruz newspapers, I would not get an unbiased accounting of what was really going on with the election. Most everything would be at least partially biased towards Cruz. The same could be said for media outlets that were Pro-Trump or Pro-Kasich.

So in the beginning I watched them all. I watched the network interviews of all the major candidates and from those interviews you got to see a bit more of who they really were. Most of the time I found the major networks were very fair to all the candidates. But I did notice that they covered some candidates that were more popular or interesting than some of the others. But we must also remember that even the new programs still need to be entertaining as well as informative.

Though this is not meant as a commercial for them but one of the most useful sources for information that I have found has been CNN. Not only can you get news and information 24/7 they almost always have multiple people on their shows to provide multiple opinions. For example they will have a Pro-Trump supporter or spokesman on with a Pro-Cruz spokesperson. This way the public gets more than one view on the subject.

I also found the hosts to be fairly unbiased although every so often something shows through for a short time when something controversial or unpopular is said. But by and large I think they really do try to present the news and the elections in a predominantly unbiased fashion. If you want only positive things said about your candidate or only negative things said about the others, CNN is not the place for you to go.

One thing I also like about some of the television media is that they are starting to question candidates more and hold them more accountable for what they say. They have also started to clamp down on evasiveness and endless political answers disguised as answers to questions. This helps give you the information you need without a lot of the rhetoric and evasiveness politicians are well-known for.

There are a few programs that I refuse to watch because I detest them and as I talk about them you probably will realize which ones these are or will notice them when you watch them. These are the shows that are not as interested in delivering the news as they are about creating controversy or getting a controversial soundbite. I do not want to see candidate or other people badgered or hounded into delivering entertaining or wrong statements because they are not given the opportunity to think before they speak. But that's just me. A lot of people like these programs.

I do not like or enjoy programs where the show or the people that run the show try to script the content or direct the people or person being interviewed to a specific answer or try to trip them up. I like to have an open and honest exchange of information and sometimes that is difficult if not impossible to achieve.

I am frustrated and interested at the same time when it comes to how people respond to the same issue. I have noted on several occasions that the seemingly rational responses are thrown out the window in favor of the "spun" versions that better fit the situation from that candidate's point of view.

But the media is now starting to openly, sometimes very aggressively, challenge these statements and that has both increased the entertainment value along with providing more useful and accurate information. They are not just allowing things to go unchallenged anymore and that is good. They have a couple of reasons for doing this. One of those reasons is creating entertainment for their viewers or readers.

The problem with the media is that it is very strongly ratings driven which means that these shows are interested in more than just providing information. They are also focused on increasing their readership or viewers and for that they need to be more interesting, more entertaining and more controversial. As we mentioned before, this often meant covering certain candidates far more than others.

The role the media plays in an election cannot be understated or undervalued. It is from these media sources that we learn about the various candidates, what they stand for and how others view them. But in this we have to be careful because we learn through the views and values of others which can taint the overall message considerably.

But the fact is that radio, television and print media are how we get and remain informed and how we get the information we need to might informed decisions. Not everyone can attend a rally or go to where the candidates are to hear and see them personally. More and more events are more media opportunities than for actually reaching the voters at the event.

Another thing that I noticed was how difficult it was to find accurate and even somewhat unbiased information on the internet. Of course you can always go to the network websites but then you get the same info that you watched on television but as far as finding information on other sites and blogs it was a very hit and miss experience.

I also found the same problem or issue with Social Media as well although on has to expect that. If someone posts or tweets or otherwise makes any kind of entry on a Social Media site their individual preferences and biases are bound to show through.

And that is perfectly OK. But I sometimes wonder if people are taking what they read as the truth or if they really stop and think that this information is coming from someone who is expressing their own thoughts and ideas as they see them and this is not always truthful or even accurate.

As in other events in life, the politicians rely on people not thinking too deeply or researching what they see and here on the internet. This is where candidates who constantly spin the facts to suit or match their agenda hope their message falls. They want people to read something, not challenge it and accept it as the truth. Unfortunately this happens far too often than it should these days.

When it comes to choosing a media source to get information, this is a highly personalized process. Not everyone likes every show and what I really like you might have a hard time watching or listening. The entertainment aspect of these shows are highly personalized as well. We need to find somewhere that we can get the accurate information we desire in a format we find interesting and enjoyable.

We put our own personalities and values into our choices as well. I mentioned that I am not someone who enjoys a hardball or confrontational program but there are a lot of people who enjoy that kind of format. This is not to say that one person is right while the other is wrong. We are all different and because of this will identify with different media outlets and resources.

It is just my hope that we choose our media resources carefully and not accept anything at face value. Look at everything further down than just on the surface and make sure it sounds reasonable and makes at least some kind of sense. Then go somewhere else or listen to someone else to see how they might feel about the same subject. You will either get your opinion confirmed or you might just get your eyes opened a bit.

Either way is just fine.

Demonstrations & Protests

Another area of interest when it comes to this primary season is the continued use of protest, both violent and non-violent when the candidates, mostly Trump, were either speaking or holding events. As the primaries went on these protest appeared to become more frequent, and at times, more violent.

Protests themselves are not unique as people are more and more vocal about their causes and beliefs. They are not even new to politics as there have been protests at political events and elections going back decades. But the difference with today's protest is that they are being covered more in-depth through the 24 hour news channels and through social media.

Today everyone has a cell phone which means everyone has the ability to instantaneously create a video, record audio or take pictures of what is happening and have them posted online in seconds. So while the actual events might seem new and unique, they are not.

As we already said, most of the protest and disruptions have occurred at Trump events. This is hardly a shock as Trump has made most of the controversial and supposedly not politically correct comments. His comments about certain races or ethnic origins of people and immigration have sparked outrage and discontent among a lot of ethnic groups.

To make matter worse, during the first protests, which were a few individuals within the Trump events, Trump had these people removed and made comments such as "I'd like to punch him in the face" or "Go ahead and punch him. I'll pay your legal bills" and other comments. While these were said pout of male bravado or to stir up and entertain the crowd or whether Trump actually meant those things was not important. Many people took those comments as tacit approval for behaving violently.

At least one such response was captured on video as a Trump supporter sucker punched a protester as he was being lead out of the building.

This was one of the first violent episodes that Trump was blamed for inciting. They increased afterwards as the protesting groups became larger and larger.

While I agree that Trump did little to nothing about stopping these responses or to lighten the mood of the crowd, I do feel like he is getting a little too much blame for the actions of people who are not Trump supporters. As for asking them to stop or calm down, if you are talking to people who are not on your side how much will they actually listen to you in the first place?

The latest protest was held in California and the protesters blocked off roads, broke through barriers, hassled police, attacked police cars and went after Trump supporters. One Trump supporter was shown with a bloody face and several protesters were arrested. They even had to chain the doors to the venue shut from the inside to keep protesters from entering the building! There are three problems with these types of protests and both of them cannot be blamed on trump.

First, while orderly protests are legal within this country no one has the right to keep another person from delivering their own message and exercising their own first amendment rights. You don't have to agree with someone but you have to allow them to speak without threats or violence or disturbing them.

Second, from what is evident on the videos of several of these disturbances and protests, it was the anti-Trump people causing the violence and most of the trouble. While I am sure that in some cases Trump supporters were part of the fighting and other violence, there was never any indication that Trump supporters started any of the altercations.

Third, and I am not saying this was the case in these incidents because I have no first-hand knowledge to back this up but there will always be people looking for a reason to disrupt anything or protest just to cause trouble or get on camera. I noticed at one of the earlier Trump rallies a group of very young people being escorted out and they were laughing and joking like it was all a lot of fun. They did not appear outraged or motivated by cause.

It is also possible, and since this is politics I would not put it past anyone that these people were sent to various locations to start trouble to give a candidate a bad name or bad press. Trump pointed out that some of these groups had professionally made signs the same type and size of one of the other candidates. He claimed this was proof that this was an organized group sent there to cause trouble. An interesting theory but nothing has come to light as yet to back that up.

I find it interesting how all the candidates are quick to condemn these kinds of actions at their opponent's rallies but are equally quick to dismiss them when they happen at their own rallies. It is a real double standard which unfortunately is quite common in politics.

I also would like to note that there are Super PAC's out for the sole purpose of discrediting and stopping Trump for whatever reasons they may have. One of the ways they do this is by fanning the flames and manufacturing information designed to inflame the people and get them to act.

If you stop for a moment and really think about it, Trump has been accused of fostering an attitude of hate and discrimination. But if you look at what Trump had said early on and what he says to this day is that he has a problem with countries who send their criminals and other here illegally and the people who have entered this country illegally and have made little or no effort to change their status once they are here.

Granted he made comments about Mexicans and he used a sweeping generality stating all of them were criminals and rapists. He should not have said that and He was talking about a certain segment of the population. Contrary to what the liberal youth might think there are no groups of people in which all are good. There are good and bad people in every ethnic and racial group and you need to understand that.

Drugs enter this country through Mexico and they are not being brought through by nuns and law abiding citizens. The drug cartels and not being run by nice and caring people looking to make the world a better place. You need to understand that as well. So if you target the bad people in a group you are not targeting the entire group. Life is not black and white and politically correct.

I think Trump had a valid point but he used the wrong words and the wrong approach to deliver his message. To make matter worse his opponents made the comments seem even worse and they all got on their high horse and fanned the flames again by condemning the comments and pandering to their audiences.

Do I believe that Trump helped this attitude get started in the first place? Of course I do. His choice of words were foolish and irresponsible. And once you say something you cannot retract it or take it back. You have to weather the storm and try to make amends or explain yourself. The only problem is that once some people hear something, or once someone does or says something that gives people a reason to cause problems, they will take it and run with it.

I think that at least that part of it played a major part of where we find ourselves right now. I'm not sure how we can stop it but publicizing it and putting protesters on television is not helping at all.

How America & Trump Have Won Already

I ask that you read this chapter with an open mind and really think about the message that I hope to deliver. Because sometimes winning and losing are not as obvious and clear cut as they appear to be and I believe this is one of those times.

As of this writing, Trump has not won or lost the nomination and has not started his run against Hillary if indeed that is to happen. But despite not have sealed the nomination yet he has already won because I believe that he has already achieved some of his most important objectives.

For much the same reason, America has won because this entire election process, as bloody and contentious as it has been, has opened the eyes of many people and that is how change begins and that is exactly how progress is made. After all, if you change nothing, nothing changes.

Though no one can really know for sure but Trump himself, his claims of doing this for our Country and for the American people at least appear to be true and heart felt. You can disagree about the sincerity involved but I have struggled to find another reason why a 70 year old billionaire who surely isn't doing it for the money and surely doesn't need to sacrifice and problems associated with the job to run for President.

So, for the sake of just getting to the message, let's agree on the motivation for his actions. Trump is not a politician and it shows but that is why he has had the success he has had and why his role in this process is so important. It is also why no one else could have achieved what he did so far to date.

People today distrust politicians and for good reason. We have seen a huge amount of government dysfunction and gridlock over the last decade all while the American people have paid the price. Income has been stagnant as prices continued to go up. More households require both people to work and sometimes have more than one job. People are being asked or forced to do more while being paid less. And they do it, grudgingly.

At the same time they see the people they elected fail to do their jobs and fail to help ease the burden on the people.

They see these politicians with their Cadillac health plans and all expenses paid lifestyle and they are angry. They see themselves making all the sacrifices while no sacrifices are being made in Washington or anywhere in government.

Because of all of this they are not listening to politicians because they correctly assume that they are part of the system that is dysfunctional and part of the problem instead of the solution. They see Cruz, Bush, Rubio and even Christie and Kasich as part of the so-called establishment that will say anything to get re-elected but do little to make the system better and more trustworthy.

They have seen the extremely poor voting records of Cruz and Rubio and they wonder if they performed at the same level if they would still have a job. It is a fair question and a fair opinion to have when everything is functioning at such a poor level. The people understand that change is needed but they do not trust someone who is part of the problem to lead that change. They figure they need someone from the outside.

We had candidates from the "outside" in Ben Carson, Carly Firorino and Donald Trump. The only candidate with any political experience if you can call losing two prior state elections experience was Fiorino. Ben Carson was a surgeon and Donald Trump was a businessman. Hardly part of the political system and in the eyes of the people, not part of the problem.

But the problem anyone has when they try to change the status quo is getting people to start listening to them. Fiorino had a big problem getting voters to listen to her and that is the main reason she had to leave the race so early in the process. She just couldn't gain any traction.

Ben Carson, the neurosurgeon, had other problems. He seemed very nice and very calm but you had a hard time picturing him in the role of president. While he was nice, many people saw him as too nice and with little direct experience that would translate into the role of President. For these reasons and probably a few more he never gained much traction either although he did do a lot better than Fiorino in that regard.

That left Trump and he had the personality to both inform and entertain and he got people to listen if not for the wrong reasons at first but he got people to listen to him. Let's face it, in life the controversial people get the coverage and Trump knew this from being on television, understanding ratings and from his experiences in business. He understood that the quiet guy in the room doesn't get much attention paid to him. But the loud and controversial guy gets attention and gets ratings.

He also did something very important in that he was not afraid to take on the Republican system which up until this year had quietly taken on a more influential role while at the same time diminishing the value of the individual vote. While this had been going on for year it was Trump who managed not only to bring it out for discussion but did so in a very open and obvious way so that it could not be quietly dealt with and allowed to continue.

He was able to do this because the party had nothing to hold over him or threaten him with. Other candidates, the so-called "lifetime or career" politicians have to think not only about what is going on today but also how their stances or positions and their comments will effect their political careers in the future. In other words, if they don't go along with what the party wants today, their future with the party could be over tomorrow. And don't think that doesn't happen.

I purposely wrote this book now rather than waiting until after the election because I think there has been so much interesting and potential life changing things happening already that we do not have to wait for the election to determine whether or not Trump's campaign or candidacy was worthwhile and whether he accomplished or won anything for the American people.

I think people get inspired when people stand up for things they believe in. This country has a long list of people who stood up for causes and issues and who took an unpopular or sometimes even dangerous stand on a sensitive issue. As we said before this is how change begins and we need more of this kind of behavior not less of it.

It takes certain strength to change something that has been part of our culture and government for so long. It takes more than standing in a group protesting and then going home to leave someone else to make the changes. That is why I think that no matter what may happen between now and the convention and the general election, the country will be changed for the better moving forward.

Topics that were once hushed or considered taboo are now being freely discussed throughout the country. Immigration, trade deals and deficits, government waste and corruption are now being talked about because people like Trump were not afraid to bring these subjects up in news conferences and debates.

We talked about protests and disruption at Trump rallies and events and I am not only not surprised that this happened but are somewhat amazed that there hasn't been more of that kind of activity.

Not because it is deserved but because over time we have seen protests and disruption whenever change is needed or attempted.

Things are the way they are because someone or some organization benefits from having things that particular way. Whenever someone speaks up or tries to change something those people stand to lose some of what they currently have and they are not happy about it. Therefore their reaction is to fight, protest or disrupt in hopes of stopping the change right then and there. Not because it is good for everyone but because it is good for them.

Over the last few months I have heard other candidate and new pundits criticize Trump for his message and his methods for delivering that message. Some of them make really valid points as we can all agree that he has said some foolish things and done some questionable things as well. But as far as bringing problems and situations out in front of the people and making them aware of what is actually going on, I think Trump has accomplished far more good than bad in his campaign. At least so far.

Think about what is likely to happen between now and the next election. There is bound to be changes in the systems on both parties that will make it more responsive to the people's vote than the party influence. There are likely going to be changes in how individual states run their primaries so there will be more uniformity throughout the country.

There are already signs that this is happening. People are demanding change and a few states have already declared that they are going to change their rules for the next election. This kind of behavior does not happen by itself. It happens only after people become aware, and sometimes outraged, when they hear of what is really going on.

And sometimes the people or person that started it all, gets no credit when the changes are actually made. Sometimes it might be months, or even years, later when all the hurdles are jumped and opposition dealt with that things change and become better. I hope that this time when the changes are made that they remember where this all started.

One last thing, and this is subject to your own feelings and perceptions. People say it was not Trump that made this all happen but all the conservative and outspoken candidates that helped bring these issues to light.

While that might be partially true, the fact is that candidates such as Rand Paul and others who mentioned some of the same issues never got any traction in the race. They spoke and maybe 3 guys in Iowa listened. Their message, or the way they delivered their message, did not resonate with the voters at anywhere near the level that Trump's message did.

Maybe it was the message, the ego, the Trump name or the way he navigated through the system but his message did get listened to for whatever reason and people did flock to the party to embrace those ideas and messages as well.

The fact is, whether you like Trump or hate him, you have to admit that his approach and personality will deliver a powerful message and cause the change he feels has to happen to take place. So if his original motives are real, that he loves this country and the people in it and wanted to help them, then he has more than accomplished his goal.

That, in a nutshell, is why Trump and America have already won.

My Apologies

I was hesitant about writing this chapter because I wrote this book from my own vantage point that was created over watching and witnessing several hundred hours of events pertaining to this election process. I did not have a specific agenda other than to inform the readers of my own observations and sometimes even revelations. So I am not sure anyone should apologize for doing just that.

At the same time I also realize that many, if not most, of the readers will think of this book as a campaign advertisement for Donald Trump. And I also understand why they might think that way. But contrary to what you might think, that was not my intention. Instead, my continued references to Trump and the things he has done were not due to his success or failure as a candidate but instead how those actions and strategies helps define the primary process this year.

Had any other candidate done exactly the same things and had the same results I would have been referencing them instead of Trump. But this year that has not been the case. This year we have seen things, and will probably continue to see even more things, that have never been seen before and that is what this book was all about. Not glorifying a specific candidate but instead looking at what happened within a campaign.

I was more interesting in the psychological issues and strategies that were used in this election than in the candidates themselves. While I guess I could have written the book without mentioning the candidates by name, it would have made it harder for people to look back or ahead and see what I talked about played out in front of them. Because of that I felt it was critical to attach names to the strategies.

We do not live in a one dimensional world where everything goes on independently of each other. Most things happen in conjunction with other things or as a direct result of something that happened earlier. Life, and these elections is more of a cause and effect than anything else and that is what has made this entire process so interesting and thought provoking at times.

Though this book is about a political system and how the candidates perform throughout this system, it is more about the psychological aspects of the process and the inequities built into the system than it is about the candidates themselves.

Because of this the candidates mentioned and used in the examples are used because of things they have personally done or reacted to throughout their campaigns.

We have seen and witnessed so much over the last several months that is likely never to been seen again and that is what makes this so interesting. Hopefully people and organizations learned from their mistakes and experiences and changes will be made to correct some of the problems within the system. At least that is what I hope will happen.

History will look back on this election for many reasons and some of them have been discussed in this book not just because they happened but why they happened in the first place. Looking back into something in real depth can make what transpires clearer and easier to understand.

And that is the basic goal here when it comes to politics and this year's election. To get people to really think about what they see and hear and understand more accurately what is happening and why it is happening. Because only then can we make progress and change the right things for the right reasons and move forward in the right direction.

Doing Your Part

People read this book for several reasons. They are either Pro-Trump or Anti-Trump and they have some level of interest in the political system. They are either outraged at the current system or merely curious as to how things really work and why things work in that manner. It doesn't really matter why you are reading this book. What matters is what you do moving forward that really counts.

The world is full of different types of people. Some of us are people who point out things that need to be changed and let others to the heavy lifting to bring that change into reality. Others use change to advance their own personal agenda and for their own personal good. Other yet use change as a reason to act out, caused trouble, incite violence and justify illegal or anti-social behavior.

But making things better, or fairer does not happen by just highlighting the problem. Change does not happen by a single or isolated incident. Instead change happens when several people step up and speak out or take action towards a common goal. That is how progress is made and society is improved.

Many people think that they are powerless or have a small voice when it comes to speaking out against or supporting a particular issue. But the truth is the voice of the people when used properly can be a powerful motivator when it comes to facilitating change.

But even when their voices might appear to fail or appear insufficient to get anyone to really listen to them, when it comes to politics they have another voices that can force people, especially politicians to pay attention and listen. Something that might be ignored for the short-term but cannot be ignored long-term.

That something is their vote.

One of the problems with the so-called "super-delegates" and "unbound delegates" is that they dilute the power of the individual vote. They lurk in the background to do the will of the party or to help facilitate back room deals to accomplish specific goals that often are not in the best interests of the people.

But rather than just give up there are things you and I and our friends and neighbors can do to help turn the tide and change the future. Things that cannot be controlled by the special interests or either party. We can exercise our power to vote and elect people we honestly feel will represent our interests instead of their own or the government.

It is amazing how there are some politicians who are well known to be puppets of the special interests or that use the power of their office for personal gain of one form or another. Yet the people elect these same people for term after term. Then they complain about the people they just elected.

We have even had candidates under investigation and found guilty re-elected. Candidates who have been found to be drug users re-elected to their offices and other problems that are magically forgotten 20 minutes after they have happened. Why people continue to do this baffles me to this day.

There is another group of people that seems to have grown over the year at least until this year and that is the group of people who have become some angry or frustrated that they just refuse to vote anymore. They see no candidate that is any different and they see how their government is performing as something that simply is not worth changing or participating in any longer. So they don't vote and the same people are re-elected again.

What I would like to ask everyone reading this book, no matter which candidate you support or which party you are affiliated with, please take a stand for whatever you believe in. You do not have to justify your views, just use the power of your vote to make a stand or voice your opinion.

Whether you are liberal or conservative, Republican or Democrat or Independent, use your vote. Support those who share your views. Not with protests or violence but by walking into that voter booth and casting your vote for the candidate you think will help make this nation better and stronger. Don't just sit home and hope things become better, play your role.

If you have the time and the inclination, consider volunteering for the candidate of your choice or perhaps donating to their campaign. You don't have to be a big corporation in order to make a difference. Candidates like Bernie Sanders financed their campaign on millions of small donations instead of huge corporate sponsorships. You can play an important role in this way as well. Think about doing that if you can.

I also would ask you to not accept things on face value. While this is a cynical view of the system, you just cannot accept the words that are coming out of a candidate's mouth. There is just too much outright lying and spinning to believe everything that you hear. Questions what you hear. Ask questions. Be the person who has to be convinced instead of the person who just follows blindly.

You do not have to believe everything a candidate says even if he is your favorite candidate.

Sometimes we believe things that change our perceptions of people only to find out what we were told was distorted or outright lies. Listen, think for a minute, and get a second or third opinion before making your decision. Everyone will thank you for that, believe me.

Last, but certainly not least, assume some responsibility for our political system. If there is something you don't like about it, speak out. If there is something you can help change, then change it. If something is wrong, make sure others know about it. If there are candidates who are not doing their job or that listen more to the special interest than they do to you and I, then vote them out and give someone else a try.

Also, be patient. Elections are held every 2-6 years depending on the position. Change usually does not happen overnight and can sometimes take decades. But this is no reason to not take the first steps right now. Because if it takes 6 years to change something and you don't start now, you are just putting those changes further out than 6 months. Take action now and make things better a little bit at a time. Slow and steady always winds the race.

Your vote is important, use it.

Your ideas are important, express them.

Your actions and support are important, give it.

If you can follow those simple rules and everyone else follows them as well, we can make a difference. But when we just sit back and let others carry the ball while we do little or nothing, nothing happens. And if we are guilty of doing nothing then we really shouldn't be allowed to complain when things do not go our way.

Please Vote!

No Matter Which Candidate You

Are Voting For,

Get Out & Vote!

It's Your Voice,

Use It!

Conclusion

There have been several times that we have looked back in history to see that events that happened back then shaped our future moving forward. Not always immediately and sometimes even far down the road but they helped shape them none the less. I think that this election process will be looked back upon as one of those times.

So many factors went into creating the election environment that we find ourselves in and many of those factors were the responsibility of the very government and politicians that are now complaining about this election. It was these feelings and the arrogance of our elected officials that created this election where the front runner is someone who may not have stood a chance otherwise.

This is also one of those elections where this is not a universally loved candidate on either side. People are scared of Trump and turned off by some of his statements and behavior. At the same time there is a universal dislike, bordering on hatred, within the party members for Ted Cruz. On the Democratic side you have Hillary who is very polarizing in her own right with her own history and baggage and Bernie Sanders who exists for many of the same reasons that Trump exists on the Republican side.

It will be interesting to see how this all plays pout in the conventions. While both Trump and Hillary seems to be the odds on favorites to win their respective nominations, it is always possible that the Republicans could go to a contested convention and then who knows what might happen if that occurs. The result there could either bring the party closer together or fracture it for good and destroy the party.

It will take time to see what will be the result of what has happened over the last few months. I'm sure there will be both good and bad but hopefully far more good than bad. Whatever happens I just hope some of what we have seen and witnessed this year will make things better and fairer to the American people moving forward.

You don't have to thank Trump for the things he has done and you don't have to agree with him or his positions on the issues. But you really do have to thank him for making certain issues and problems known by all the people instead of just a few carefully chosen insiders.